Empowered —Healing the Heartbeat of Your Family

Marilyn Howshall

Empowered—*Healing the Heartbeat of Your Family*

by Marilyn Howshall

This Book is Published by *JM Howshall Legacy, LLC*

Empowered ~ Healing the Heartbeat of Your Family

This paperback book is Copyright © 2023 Marilyn Howshall

Digital edition e-book Copyright © 2016 Marilyn Howshall

Editing has been updated, but the message hasn't changed since it was initially published under the title *Empowering the Transfer of Moral Values and Faith* Copyright © 2011 Marilyn Howshall

Unless otherwise indicated, all Scripture quotations are taken from The Amplified® Bible, Copyright © 1954, 1958, 1962, 1965, 1987 by The Lockman Foundation.

Cover Concept Art and Design by Barbie Poling

No Electronic Copying, Forwarding, or Retypesetting Permitted All Rights Reserved; Published in the U.S.A.

Empowering the Heartbeat of Your Life
www.marilynhowshall.com

Dedication

This book is dedicated to the work of the Gospel of Jesus Christ—the ministry of reconciliation—God's plan for believers described in 2 Corinthians 5:17-19, and to Empowered Hearts Community Church at Coeur d'Alene, Idaho who believe in Christ's finished work for their lives.

"Now we look inside, and what we see is that anyone united with the Messiah gets a fresh start, is created new. The old life is gone; a new life burgeons! Look at it! All this comes from the God who settled the relationship between us and Him, and then called us to settle our relationships with each other. God put the world square with Himself through the Messiah, giving the world a fresh start by offering forgiveness of sins. God has given us the task of telling everyone what He is doing. We're Christ's representatives. God uses us to persuade men and women to drop their differences and enter into God's work of making things right between them. We're speaking for Christ Himself now: Become friends with God; He's already a friend with you."

2 Corinthians 5:17-19 The Message Bible

"Therefore if any person is [ingrafted] in Christ (the Messiah) he is a new creation (a new creature altogether); the old [previous moral and spiritual condition] has passed away. Behold, the fresh and new has come! But all things are from God, Who through Jesus Christ reconciled us to Himself [received us into favor, brought us into harmony with Himself] and gave to us the ministry of reconciliation [that by word and deed we might aim to bring others into harmony with Him]. It was God [personally present] in Christ, reconciling and restoring the world to favor with Himself, not counting up and holding against [men] their trespasses [but canceling them], and committing to us the message of reconciliation (of the restoration to favor)."

2 Corinthians 5:17-19 AMP

With Deep Gratitude

It is with deep gratitude that God, in His wondrous grace and favor, saw fit to perform such marvelous works in the midst of, what was in my personal life, a lengthy season of chronic trials and suffering. A family allowed me the honor of working closely in their lives in cooperation with the nudgings and instruction of the Holy Spirit to bring about whole-life change. You will be getting to know them throughout this book. Tim and Barbie Poling came to believe in this message for themselves, live it, and help their children live by it too. I was blessed to witness many, many miracles of reconciliation and even freedom from strongholds, and the continued work of the Holy Spirit to form Christlike character. I'm humbly indebted to *Empowered Hearts Community Church*, and I continue to be deeply grateful for their presence in my life.

When, being led by the Holy Spirit, I brought the truth first to Barbie, she listened, took it to the Lord, received His correction and instruction, and obeyed. She reconciled with her mom who was in an advanced stage of Alzheimer's, helped her mom reconcile her life to family members and to Jesus. She influenced her children, and next her husband to also listen to the correction of the Holy Spirit. I was blessed to see it all up close, and it seemed at the time that miracles just tumbled all over themselves in their rush to get to the Poling family. Their testimonies are now part of this book, as well as "Ellen's Story" as told by her daughter, Barbie. Barbie and Tim continue to reach out to other families in our local community, setting a great example while helping them to reconcile their lives to Christ.

Barbie wanted to see this book finished and published, and so she tackled the huge job of helping me give it the additional attention it needed to make it available to you. Barbie became my dear friend and co-laborer first in ministry and now also in business. She has been and continues to be a blessing to my life from the Lord Himself. There are no words within my grasp to express my heart-felt feelings for her. She's precious to Jesus and to me.

Contents

Introduction	X
1. Our Failure to Transfer Moral Values and Faith to Our Children	1
2. Moral Clarity ~ Christ's Law of Love	13
3. Instilling Moral Values at the Heart Level	31
4. Our Purpose ~ Learning to Love Much and Well	49
5. Calling Relational Immorality What It Is ~ Sin	67
6. A Return to Conscience	91
7. God's Top-Down, Inside-Out Approach to Parenting	117
8. The Price to Form Moral Character	133
9. The Ministry of Reconciliation	151
Information	184
Glossary Appendix	186
Scripture Appendix	192
Author's Biography	194

My Stories & Polings' Testimonies

6   Chapter 1 — My Story ~ *"Quite Telling ~ The Emperor's New Clothes"*
9   Polings' Testimonies

25   Chapter 2 — My Story ~ *"At the Core"*
27   Polings' Testimonies

39   Chapter 3 — My Story ~ *"What a Mess!"*
41   Polings' Testimonies

56   Chapter 4 — My Story ~ *"Becoming Real ~ The Velveteen Rabbit"*
58   My Story ~ *"Course Corrections"*
63   Polings' Testimonies

70   Chapter 5 — My Story ~ *"The Fog Lifts"*
83   Polings' Testimonies

95   Chapter 6 — A Personal Example *~ The Wrong Approach to Self-Evaluation*
105   My Story ~ *"Shocked into Silence"*
106   A Personal Story of Ministry *~ "Jumpstarting a Conscience"*
109   Polings' Testimonies

117   Chapter 7 — My Story ~ *"An Ill Fit"*
124   My Story *~ "Becoming Parented All Over Again"*
128   Polings' Testimonies

134 Chapter 8 — My Story ~ ***"Staking My Claim"***
135   My Story ~ ***"Forming My Family's Morality"***
145   Polings' Testimonies

Introduction

I've seen them everywhere—the devastating effects of children abandoning their parents' values and faith as they grow up—broken hearts, broken relationships, broken lives. The evidence abounds, and the fruit of it begins when children are still living at home: bickering between siblings, dislike or disdain subtly or openly expressed between siblings, irritation expressed in emotional distance and facial features, punishing gestures with body language, frustration expressed in angry outbursts, resistance to instruction, teens acting out against their parents' wishes. All of these behaviors are commonly and regularly seen in churches showing the true condition of the heartbeat of average Christian families. Individuality and independence are qualities parents want for their children, but these common behaviors often send their children in the direction of self-centeredness and individualism, which gives parents cause for concern.

A national survey done by the Barna Group found that "fewer than two out of every ten Christian parents believe they are doing a good job of training their children morally and spiritually." Clearly, Christian parents don't understand what moral and spiritual training consists of and are leaving it to chance. Yes, we've lost our way, but you don't have to become part of these sad statistics. You can find your way back. My husband and I did, and other parents we know are also allowing God to parent them at the heart level. Some have learned how to reach their children's hearts for the Lord while maintaining an unbroken Christlike influence with their children. Others are in various stages of learning how resulting in miracles of reconciliation in their families. You can learn God's ways too!

This book answers the question: *How can we as parents effectively transfer our moral values and faith to our children, forming moral character in them while at the same time promoting true discipleship to Christ?* Expanding on eight challenging ideas, I clarify what true biblical morality is, how it is developed, and the relational environment needed to instill biblical morality in our children. I define often misunderstood biblical words and expose commonly held false ideas that may be unknowingly keeping you from the life-changing spiritual growth you want to instill in your children. I share with you how God wants to work in your life to equip you to effectively train your children's moral character toward Christlike righteousness.

Throughout the book I share my own testimony of how God got my attention, gave me moral clarity, and taught me how to pass it to my children, forming true Christlike character in them. At the end of each chapter, you will follow the story of another couple, Tim and Barbie Poling, who came to understand what God wanted to do in them and chose to cooperate so they could turn around the moral culture of their home. Today they are successfully transferring their moral values and faith to their children.

This subject promises to be eye-opening and life-changing for all serious Christians, parents, young couples, and single adults whose desire is to embody the principles of the Gospel of Jesus Christ. His influence in your heart and life will transform you into an effective influence in the hearts and lives of others, beginning with your own precious children. The message of this book will educate your conscience and raise your standard for following Christ as it points the way for authentic Christian living. It also informs you of actions to take now to become better parents. Equipped with new understanding of how God works in you, He will empower you to heal the heartbeat of your family.

Chapter 1

Our Failure to Transfer Moral Values and Faith to Our Children

~ Challenging Idea and Sobering Reality #1 ~
"Most Christian parents don't know what moral and spiritual training consists of and are leaving it to chance."
~ You are being told on by your own relational fruit, but the hope is that God wants to empower you to change your fruit.

The previous statement will seem bold and even presumptuous to some reading this, but it needs to be said, nevertheless. The Church is failing miserably in our God-given mandate to raise up our children for the Lord and His purposes, and it's my intention to show you why I believe this is so.

As Christians, we believe that faith and morality are supposed to be instilled in children. However, it *seems* like the morality of parents has not been transferred from one generation to the next. In fact, our moral culture has been in a steady decline for the last several decades. I suggest that our definition of morality and a true biblical moral standard have been lost to the culture of family and church in this country, along with the process of relational discipleship, which alone can facilitate the transfer of morality and faith to children and adult believers alike.

The statistics regarding the condition of the church are quite alarming, and cannot be refuted. The statistics tell us that while we may not be failing to church our children and tell them about God, and that we may not be failing to transfer some sort of values to them, we certainly *are* failing to transfer *biblical* moral values and faith to them so they will choose God and relate with Him on His terms. Extensive research bears this out—that our fruit is telling on us. We have to ask, what's happening?

Not many like to listen to statistics, and we don't really need them to prove what's happening since the fruit is already telling on the church, but I want to shock us to awareness because most Christian parents are unknowingly participating in fueling some of the problems.

Research on Parenting

George Barna is said to be one of the most often quoted men in the nation, authoring more than 35 books, including Revolution, Boiling Point, and Revolutionary Parenting, and is the founder of the Barna Group, a research and resource firm.[1] He found more than 75,000 different parenting books currently at our disposal. It seems like overkill, but it suggests a need.

Barna examined the titles and subtitles of the 100 best-selling books on the market and dug beneath the surface to identify a significant weakness in the literature. His conclusion: virtually every book is based upon

---

1. The Barna Group's clients have ranged from ministries such as the Billy Graham Association and Focus on the Family to corporations such as Ford and Walt Disney, as well as the U.S. Navy and U.S. Army. For this book alone (Revolutionary Parenting) the Barna Group compiled data from a series of surveys after conducting thousands of interviews with parents and young adults to show the church what it takes to develop strong parental influence and produce children who walk in real faith in God.

personal observations, experiences, or assumptions. They promote a particular point of view or parenting strategy but typically ignore the motivation for engaging in parenting in the first place.

> *"The implied motivation is that parents should raise their child simply because the child exists and the parents are responsible for that reality. There is rarely any recognition of the fact the child is a special gift and raising children is a responsibility assigned to parents by God. As such, parenting bears an innate importance and an irrefutable connection to parenting principles furnished by God."*
> George Barna, Revolutionary Parenting

He continues by saying that while parents may agree that moral and spiritual development equips a child for life, they are divided nearly down the middle as to who is responsible for this training. Moreover, another survey shows that of the half who do believe they are most responsible for their children's spiritual development, nearly half of these parents do not consider their own faith among the most important influences on their parenting practices. Certainly, this is a contradiction and also tells us that fewer than 25% of Christian parents are influencing their children's faith toward God.

> *"While parents may agree that moral and spiritual development equips a child for life, they are divided nearly down the middle as to who is responsible for this training."*

Here is just a sampling of the survey's conclusions of a nationally representative sample of children between the ages of eight and twelve: *"Most churched children are biblically illiterate and become part of the 64% of churched adolescents who don't believe the Bible is accurate in all of the principles it teaches."*

This means the children are left to their own resources to form their own morality, which in turn leads them into relational, intellectual, and possibly political error.

Here's another: *"Salvation baffles most churched children. Only 2 out of 10 reject the idea good people can earn their way into heaven. Only 3 out of 10 dismiss the belief that everyone experiences the same post-death outcome, regardless of their beliefs."* These statistics are coming from Christian homes. Surely you can realize these kids who are being raised by parents claiming the Christian faith are not saved. They do not understand what sin is or their need to be forgiven, and they do not possess an eternal perspective.

And another: *"More than half believe Jesus Christ sinned while He lived on earth and two-thirds contend He didn't return to physical life after His crucifixion and death on the cross."* This means they can reject any standard for righteousness that is put before them, and develop a view about the Christian faith that lumps it in with all other religions, rendering Christ's sacrifice on the cross and His resurrection powerless to change their lives.

Add to this the fact that: *"More than half of the 13-year-olds in churches think they already know everything of significance in the Bible."* This indicates they received a superficial transference of knowledge and information only through words that didn't contribute to the heart-level growth that would align them rightly with God and with doctrinal truth. It also means they are no longer open to learning or actively pursuing the knowledge of God.

Also, consider that: *"Fewer than 2 out of every 10 Christian parents believe they are doing a good job of training their children morally and spiritually. In fact, on a national survey, parents rated their effectiveness lower on these two areas of performance than on any of the 15 areas they were asked to address."*

This tells me that *most* Christian parents don't understand what moral and spiritual training consists of and are leaving it to chance. We can clearly expect more than eight out of every ten Christian parents to fail in transferring biblical moral values and faith to the next generation. One reason we can say we are failing is that parents themselves are telling us they don't understand how to do it! Could it be that the parents in our churches need to become truly discipled? What a shocking thought, considering the church as a whole thinks they are actuality discipling believers!

~Sobering Reality~
You are being told on by your own relational fruit.

If it's true that adults haven't been properly discipled, then they have to find a way to deal with the guilt about failing their children. Perhaps they find solace in colluding with the other parents who fall into the 80 percent group who don't believe they are doing a good job of training their children morally and spiritually. They silently agree by adopting and sympathizing with "false confessions" to assuage their guilt. This certainly must lead to seeking out substitute gospels to serve in order to feel right, but it's at the expense of forming Christlike character toward true spiritual growth in themselves and their children.

Let me give an example of false confessions. Many behaviors common to teenagers are considered to be "normal" and to be expected, such as self-centeredness, and so parents agree together that this is a normal phase for that age group. Even the experts say so! The reality is that the behaviors are only common to those who have never been discipled at the heart level, leaving self-centeredness in place to continue developing a stronger hold on the child. Believers are left to walk in their own wisdom, perpetuating personal lies that are contrary to the Gospel of Christ. As Barna said, these realities can be somewhat frightening for the future of our children, our church, and our culture.

It appears there has been a steady progression toward a wholesale abandoning of parental responsibility, leading to the prevention of our children's spiritual maturity, which is nothing less than—spiritual abortion. When the vast majority of Christian parents, even if unknowingly, abort the spiritual maturity of their own children, it's easy to see why infant abortion ever gained ground in the first place. We can't influence the outside if the inside hasn't been influenced and changed first. I know this is a hot issue, and I'm not blaming anyone in particular here. I understand that we all have been caught in a culture and times in which we were reared. We learned to trust in the superficial, knowledge-based parenting and discipling models offered to us that circumvented relational heart-based training. We were taught that knowledge (instead of a changed heart) would make true believers and followers of Christ, and we were further taught that it's easy to give that task of transferring knowledge to our children to other people. This freedom allowed for the perceived need of both parents to work outside the home. However, it doesn't let us off the hook as far as God's relational model of parenting that requires parents to be present to their children. At some point we can choose, that if He has an objective for us and our family then He also has the way to show us how to journey toward living it out.

> *"Could it be that the parents in our churches need to become truly discipled? What a shocking thought, considering the church as a whole thinks they are in actuality discipling believers!"*

Personal Story ~ "Quite Telling ~ The Emperor's New Clothes"

My siblings and I sometimes engaged in bratty behavior with each other when we were growing up. If one child did something wrong, another would go "tell" on the offender. It wasn't always the offended who would tell; it could be any one of us seven kids. "Telling on someone" was always viewed as a bad thing to do—like a betrayal of trust. After all, we were supposed to protect each other in our "secret" sins, but instead, we betrayed the very ones we were all in cahoots with. As a church, these statistics reveal that we are being told on, but instead of exposing sin we collude with each other to justify and excuse ourselves that our bad spiritual fruit is to be expected, "For after all," we say, "They're just children," or "They're just going through a normal phase" or "Parenting is hard work," and worse yet, "Everyone is the same way."

Who hasn't heard the classic metaphor, The Emperor's New Clothes about the emperor's vanity, which led him to be deceived by his own clothing designers' trickery? The idea, that we think we are clothed a certain way when in fact we are not, is profoundly applicable to our "Christian" parenting. Here is my version:

> *Christians have a silent agreement with one another, putting on—like a cloak—an appearance of faith and righteousness with church activities or lifestyle values, believing the lie they have God's favor and are producing godly fruit. In reality, their homes are in relational chaos, family members each grasping for their own selfish way in relational unlove. The real fruit of their relationships tells on them, betraying their "Christianized" nakedness. Just like the child who innocently tells the truth about the Emperor's nakedness, it is God's children—authentic Christians—who expose the nakedness of the church simply by the fruit of Christlike character that is expressed in real and selfless love for one another.*

Betrayed and Led Astray

The statistics are alarming and quite telling. The research is betraying the fact that much of what we do in the privacy of our homes is comprised of sin—disobedience to God and His Moral Law of Love—His relational value system. God mercifully warns us that *"for whatever a man sows, that and that only is what he will reap"* (Galatians 6:7 AMP).

Friends, this means we don't need anyone to tell on us. God warned us that our own fruit would tell on us, and fruit isn't something we can hide! Our own marriages and children reflect on our true spiritual condition more than we know, and now we are reaping the destructive results of our false value system. The church has been led astray, but you as a parent can find your way back. God has a way for us if we will take heed and follow His instruction. Statistics aren't life's operating laws; they can be changed as long as we are willing to change our course.

People don't usually mind being reminded they are sinners, as long as they're not asked to look at their *particular* sin and tell the truth about how it hurts those who matter the most to them. The church fosters the notion that righteousness and morality are separate from relationships. However, in God's book, morality and righteousness are all about relationships. God's plan for our development in righteousness includes our understanding of *how* we sin in our primary relationships so we can experience the conviction that works toward repentance and reconciliation. Only then can we receive God's grace and forgiveness to put matters right between us and God, and between us and the important people in our lives. It is this heart-level repentance that aligns us correctly with Him where He has an open door into our lives for powerful works of grace toward Christlike character formation.

> "There is a way which seems right to a man and appears straight before him, but at the end of it is the way of death." ~ Proverbs 14:12 AMP

The object of this book's message is to correct our failure to understand true biblical morality. We will be taking a look at what morality actually is and attempting to answer this question: *How can we effectively transfer our moral values and faith to our children, forming moral character in them while at the same time promoting true discipleship to Christ?* Are you confident that your children will choose God and learn to relate with Him correctly as their Father while living their lives in service to Jesus Christ? The following messages will help you find your way.

A Merciful Reminder ~*You are being told on by your own relational fruit, but the hope you have in Christ is that God wants to empower you to change your fruit!*

Testimonies

Barbie describes some of the truths she had to tell about her relational fruit.

> *I needed to tell the truth about many things: I used my children for my own image. I flaunted my talents and knowledge in order to get approval. I did not know God, and I was serving a false image of God that I had created with my own mind. I allowed people to manipulate and control me, and I even wanted them to do so. I was losing my children's hearts as they entered their teen years. I was placing my children in situations where they were developing false personalities. I was contributing to and enabling my husband to remain trapped in his sin. I took God's place as the judge in my life and lived in self-condemnation.*

Barbie describes what she was attempting to teach her children through previous discipling efforts and if it affected their hearts.

> *I wanted my children to be discipled to the Lord. As a homeschooler, I had nearly daily discussions with them over Scripture. I tried my best to apply what we read to their particular lives, often focusing on the Proverbs, and sporadically helping them to memorize Scripture. In our church attendance, I oversaw what they were learning by being present or being the teacher in their classes. I taught them a lot about the Bible and the history contained in the Bible. We required them to pray at a family gathering before bed each night. As they got older, I tried to encourage them to have their own devotional time in which they read their Bibles and briefly journaled their prayers and thanksgiving. We also occasionally used a character curriculum to work on some assignments pertaining to particular*

undesirable behaviors. This consisted of some Scripture memory, some study of biblical characters with the desired behavior, and journal entries about the current behavior and the more desirable behavior.

At home, I helped them to work through conflicts with each other and keep themselves from being unkind. I worked with them to serve and to perform their duties without complaint. There were a few issues of quiet disrespect and resistance that I didn't know how to change. I felt helpless to change them using the methods I always depended upon because the issues were of a deeper nature than simple obedience and control of their words. I was unhappy with this quiet disrespect and resistance, and my unhappiness caused them to feel my disapproval of them. I didn't really feel like being affectionate with them because of this underlying distance so I was much less affectionate.

8 Challenging Ideas and Corresponding Sobering Realities

Challenging Idea #1 ~ *Most Christian parents don't know what moral and spiritual training consists of and are leaving it to chance.*

Sobering Reality #1 ~ *You are being told on by your own relational fruit, but the hope is that God wants to empower you to change your fruit.*

It Starts with You

Your Heavenly Father is loving, personal, and intimate. He already has the desire to help you learn how to parent your children for Him. As you begin to allow Him to parent you first, He will teach you and guide you. He only needs one person in your family to open the door for Him to begin His best work in your life. You don't have to wait for your spouse to start. Just open your heart and say, "Yes" to Him. Are you willing to allow God to start with you? Can you say aloud to Him, "It Starts with Me, Here I am, Lord."

Chapter 2

Moral Clarity ~ Christ's Law of Love

~ Challenging Idea and Sobering Reality #2 ~
"Morality is the heart-level quality of how people relate with each other, defining character as the sum of our relational habits."
~ The state of your relationships defines your character and reflects your true spiritual condition. You are your children's character education.

While it *seems* that the moral values of parents have not been transferred to their children, our fruit doesn't lie. God warned us that our own fruit would tell on us. It is telling us that in reality our own morality *is* being transferred, producing a particular relational fruit that in turn forms character. Unfortunately, it is not always the fruit we were hoping for. The church has lost a biblical definition of morality *and* the relational context in which it is supposed to be formed. We no longer seem to comprehend the scope of what it means to be moral or immoral. There has been a definite blurring of the lines between right and wrong. Fritz Ridenour, in *The Conscience and Post-Modernism*, writes:

> *"A modern lack of commitment to absolute truth has led to a different view of the conscience on the part of many Christians. Right and wrong have been replaced by what 'feels right' or praying about some question or course of action and 'feeling good about it.'"*

We must begin to take a closer look at the nature of morality.

Cut Off from the Workings of Conscience

In most people's minds, morality has only to do with sexual behavior, due to familiar passages of Scripture where sins are mentioned, pertaining to sexual vices, such as adultery, incest, sensuality, and sodomy. Immorality is also commonly linked to societal sins, such as abortion. We subconsciously relegate the warnings against such "big" sins to the unrighteous, the unsaved, or the unchurched.

> *"In giving sin such a narrow expression, we are cutting ourselves off from the workings of conscience."*

Intellectually we know we sin, but we think immorality doesn't apply to the common Christian, because "we" don't do such things. In giving sin such a narrow expression, we are cutting ourselves off from the workings of conscience. We simply don't recognize sin's influence in our hearts and as it's expressed in our relationships. The paradigm shift needed to identify our sin—our immorality—is what this chapter's message is about, and so we're going to be looking at the Moral Law of Love to bring clarity to the relational nature of forming biblical morality.

Three Common Terms that Point to The Law

We need to develop a more accurate understanding of three terms that point to the Law.

1.) Morality

Morality is about the habitual manners or conduct and personal behavior of people in relation to one another as social beings whose actions have a bearing on each other's rights and happiness, and with reference to right and wrong. And so, morality is about our customary actions in how we treat other people, whether those actions are good or bad. Since moral is a neutral word, having to do with the quality of behavior and conduct in relating with others, I like to make this simple distinction: Morality is the quality of how people relate with each other. If morality is the quality of how people relate with each other, then immorality can be detected in all of our relational patterns of behavior, and therefore is much more all-encompassing than simply sexual and societal sin.

2.) Righteousness

A common term we take for granted, righteousness is about purity of heart and rectitude of life, being conformed to the Divine Law by daily practice. And so being righteous is when we are in right standing with God's Moral Law in thought, word, and deed. While morality is a neutral word, rectitude is not. In fact, rectitude further defines the quality of morality God is after in us.

3.) Moral Rectitude

Rectitude, no longer a common word, is found only nineteen times in *The Amplified Bible* in conjunction with moral conduct and in reference to righteousness. Rectitude is conformity to the Moral Law in thought and in conduct. From the 1828 dictionary, *"The more nearly the rectitude of men approaches the standard of the Divine Law of Love, the more exalted and dignified is their character. The want of rectitude is not only sinful but debasing."* Moral rectitude is about the quality of love in the way we relate with others—our right standing with them and with God that makes us righteous. Following are three examples of how this word is used in Scripture, pointing to our relating practices.

"The way of the [consistently] righteous (those living in moral and spiritual rectitude in every area and relationship of their lives) is level and straight; You, O [Lord], Who are upright, direct aright and make level the path of the [uncompromisingly] just and righteous."

Isaiah 26:7 AMP

"...Break off your sins and show the reality of your repentance by righteousness (right standing with God and moral and spiritual rectitude and rightness in every area and relation) and liberate yourself from your iniquities by showing mercy and loving-kindness to the poor and oppressed..."

Daniel 4:27 AMP

"Stand therefore [hold your ground], having tightened the belt of truth around your loins and having put on the breastplate of integrity and of moral rectitude and right standing with God..."

Ephesians 6:14 AMP

Moral rectitude and righteousness point to the Divine Law—God's Law of Love. Many of us can easily think we walk in moral rectitude and righteousness because we carry our own definition of the Divine Law. We could think of it as the Ten Commandments or a set of societal behaviors such as hard work, modesty, orderly families, or church activity. But the Bible is very clear in its definition of the Divine Law, and through an examination of the Law, we will come to realize that we, along with the vast majority of the church, have adopted our own false notion of it, resulting in bad relational fruit in our families.

The New Testament Makes the Law About Love
~ A Closer Look

Let's look at two passages in Matthew. First, a loving warning: We've heard these passages quoted and even quote them ourselves without thinking about it. Familiar mental assent to these well-rehearsed Scriptures will hide the fact we may be failing to transfer these simple truths into our lives.

> *"You shall love the Lord your God with all your heart and with all your soul and with all your mind (intellect). This is the great (most important principle) and first commandment. And a second is like it: 'You shall love your neighbor as [you do] yourself. These two commandments sum up and upon them depend the Law and the Prophets."*
>
> Matthew 22:37-40 AMP

> *"But seek (aim at and strive after) first of all His Kingdom and His righteousness (His way of doing and being right), and then all these things taken together will be given you besides."*
>
> Matthew 6:33 AMP

These truths contain what on the surface may seem like simple ideas, but they suggest something quite powerful and far more complex than we can imagine. Let's take a closer look.

> "Morality is the quality of how
> people relate with each other."

A closer look tells us that both of these commands compel us to seek God and love Him first and foremost. Matthew 22:40 says that upon the two great commandments, the Law and the Prophets are summed up and upon them they depend. Think about this: all the Law and all the Prophets are summed up—everything God ever said He wants *from* His children—LOVE, and everything He ever promised to do *for* His children—LOVE—in a two-way relationship.

Therefore, everything God wants from us and everything He wants to do for us is conditioned on His unconditional LOVE working through us, because Scripture tells us we have none of our own. This demands our attention, for it indicates that righteousness [moral and spiritual rectitude; right living—in relationship with God and with others], and the blessings that come with it will be fulfilled in our lives only when we love God with a whole, undivided heart. The problem is, we really don't know what it means to "love God with a whole, undivided heart."

Matthew 6:33 confirms that if we attend to God's relational priorities everything else will be ours. In other words, life will work for us. The Christian life will possess the power to transform us and our families, and the blessings of God will come to us. The Lord also spelled it out very clearly in Deuteronomy, which tells us all about the blessings and cursings that would come to us depending on how we chose to live our lives, in self will [cut off from experiencing God's love and acceptance] or in God's will [experiencing His love and acceptance].

Drs. Henry Cloud and John Townsend, co-authors of *How People Grow*, are strong proponents of the formation of moral character being centered in our relationships. In fact, they say that all personal growth is spiritual growth, and that *"to solve life's problems and to grow spiritually are one and the same thing."* To reconcile our lives to Christ or as the authors put it:

> *"To return to the created order means to get back into relationship with God and with each other. As Jesus said, all of the commandments can be summed up in the two greatest commandments of loving God and loving others (Matthew 22:37-40).*
>
> *Everything in life depends on these two relationships. Redemption puts us back into those two relationships. First, it reconciles us into a relationship with God through faith and forgiveness and the re-establishing of a connection. Second, redemption*

brings us back to the rightful restoration of connectedness with others as it stresses love, identification with each other through the Golden Rule, caring for one another, forgiving one another, healing one another, teaching one another, correcting one another, and so on.

Without restoration of relationship with each other, we would still be in a state of alienation and not able to have the connections that provide the things we need to live and to grow. Redemption reverses our alienation and isolation from each other and gets us rightly reconnected."

Being rightly reconnected with others is the beginning of developing moral rectitude. The practical task is to learn new ways of relating in our family relationships so our connections become stronger, deeper, and more meaningful. The process required to form Christlike character in our relational practices will bring harmony and wholeness to our lives as God intended all along. We can conclude that <u>a life that results in receiving the blessings of the Kingdom of God is a life lived for the Lord with a whole, undivided heart, allowing His ways and His love to actually change us at the core of our being</u>. Otherwise, truth will never find its way into our relational patterns, and we will miss out on the life God has promised to His children as we experience the personal and often lonely distress of resistant, strained, or broken family relationships.

The Law is about Our Heart Activity
~ Jesus Exposes Stony Hearts

[handwritten: The L is what matters!]

God's standard of Love is the only standard by which we measure morality on the scale of bad to good behavior. Jesus demonstrates that adherence to the Divine Law is a matter of the sacrificial quality of our heart as it is outworked in relationships. Thus, moral rectitude is adherence to the Law of Love at the heart level. The Moral Law of Love is about the *quality* of our attitudes, intentions, and motivations with other people and with God.

Jesus provided a prime example saying that if a man so much as looked at another woman to lust after her, it would be the same as if he had already committed adultery with her in his heart (Matthew 5:28). While Jesus uses the example of a sexual act of sin, referencing the commandment, "Thou shalt not commit adultery," He points to where such unfaithfulness originates—in the heart. As a single act of adultery, sin's expression is narrowly and generally defined.

> *~ **Remember This!**~*
> *The state of your relationships*
> *defines your character and reflects*
> *your true spiritual condition. You are*
> *your children's character education.*

However, there are many very "particular" signs of unfaithfulness that characterize a strained or broken and unfaithful marriage relationship. Such a marriage can last for years without the spouses ever actually cheating on each other with another person. Although eventually, their unhappiness, caused by much sinning against each other, can lead to a separation either physically or emotionally. However, the signs of unfaithfulness were there all along in how the spouses treated each other in uncaring ways, such as: failing to listen, being easily offended, withholding affection and emotions, hiding things from one another, attempting to control one another, and each going their own way even while cohabiting.

The *particular* correction and instruction on how to relate in love [developing un-self-centered moral qualities in attitudes, intentions, and motivations] would have prevented the eventual downfall of the marriage. Some such marriages may never turn to actual physical adultery, but nevertheless, the sin of unfaithfulness is there just the same.

Another example of the quality of our heart is self-centered anger, which when left unchecked, can become hatred within the heart, and according to Jesus, is the same as the immorality of committing murder. The immorality can be found in the many particular self-seeking attitudes of the heart that may lead to anger, such as: taking up personal offense at the immaturity or lack of discipline in a child, fuming with frustration at interruptions to your plan, or nurturing feelings of self-pity at being misunderstood by a spouse.

Don't forget the inward denial—which is the same as the immorality of lying—of any number of sinful attitudes that need honest acknowledgment and repentance. As a form of denial, we use nice-sounding labels for behaviors that are actually rooted in sin, such as shortcomings, faults, dominant personality traits, or even hormones. These may be legitimate weaknesses in our natural makeup, but if we put nice labels on unloving relating patterns to excuse and circumvent conviction, and haven't yet allowed God to redeem our personality, then there is really no other name to call it but immorality—just plain old fleshly behavior—a carnal response or reaction of self-will that's perhaps caused by a legitimate condition of our life, but where we have a choice in how to respond. In every case, we are breaking God's Moral Law of Love.

> *"The Old Testament Moral Law was always about God's relational value system."*

By exposing the quality of our moral and spiritual rectitude [the heart-level quality of how we relate with others], Jesus is also exposing our corrupt and evil tendencies—our unsanctified hearts.

The Law Is about Relationships
~ Jesus Makes the Law Particular

Upon a surface examination of the Ten Commandments, it's easy for believers to think they are living moral lives. After all, they go to church and don't lie, cheat, steal or murder so think they must be doing all right in the righteousness department. But the Old Testament Moral Law was always about God's relational value system.

In pointing out the law-breaking hiding in people's hearts, Jesus simply exposes what God's intentions have always been, making it plain that the Law—morality—is all about the *condition* of our hearts in relation to God and to others—the quality of our attitudes, intentions, and motivations.

We are already wired through our sinful nature toward self-serving unique *attitudes* [mental or emotional posture], *intentions* [earnest bending of the mind], and *motivations* [driving force] in our hearts. Our internal heart activity forms our relating habits and patterns and dictates our relational health. All of our pre-disposed responses to other people were formed in childhood when we weren't with our parents and were left to find ways to build defenses against being hurt, rejected, manipulated, misunderstood, and so on. Without a parent's vigilant attention and instruction, no child will possess the inner strength and the many needed proper responses to outward stimuli. The result is the forming of a self-serving false personality that covers up the true self, turning the character away from becoming Christlike.

> *"LOVE's evidence [God's standard for moral fruit] is seen in the sacrificial quality of the heart-level attitudes, intentions, and motivations of our relating practices."*

The amazing truth is that children can grow up to become young adults who are mature in their relating habits and practices, mature in their character, and able to make wise and healthy relational decisions—true to their real personality and true to Christlike qualities. They simply need Christlike parenting where parents have allowed God to parent them first.

Jesus was always pointing to our need for an intimate relationship with the Father so we could receive the *particular* correction and instruction we needed in order for our hearts and lives to embody His Law of Love. He wants our stony hearts to receive the finger-writing of God's Law of Love, which is a far better plan than the first one, which could only address righteousness in *general, narrowly*-defined ways (Hebrews 8:6).

Jesus *broadened* and made very *particular* the definition of the Divine Law of Love: True Christlike moral character [righteousness] is laying down one's life for others. This includes laying down self-perceived rights, defenses, making assumptions, and learning how to extend a gracious benefit of the doubt, and making intentional efforts to understand others. Immorality [sin] includes everything that is unloving and out of self-centered motivations at someone else's expense, such as resentment, emotionally withdrawing, irritation, harshness, perfectionism, forced unity or forced submission, jealousy, and taking up offenses—just to name a few. In short, all these activities are unloving and immoral, which identifies sin simply as a failure to love. And so, simply stated, *LOVE's evidence [God's standard for moral fruit] is seen in the sacrificial quality of the heart-level attitudes, intentions, and motivations of our relating practices.*

> **"ATTITUDE** ~ The mental or
> emotional posture that
> expresses your sentiments
> and actions"

The Law of Love Is Not About Hiding Out in Religion

Many believers hide out under the broad generalities of the Old Testament Law of Righteousness (morality), by doing "good works" while keeping their hearts closed to God's work. An example is when they excuse their harshness and controlling behaviors because they believe it produces outward compliance in children, making their family appear to be righteous. Remember, God is working in our lives according to His law of love. If you hold to any other thinking, you will be in serious delusion and possess a false sense of security, because you will be rejecting the work of Christ. The Apostle Paul warned against such as those who chose to remain under the old law.

> "For [although] they hold a form of piety (true religion), they deny and reject and are strangers to the power of it [their conduct belies the genuineness of their profession]. Avoid [all] such people [turn away from them]."
>
> 2 Timothy 3:5 AMP

A Practical Working Definition of Morality

These truths possess practical implications for creators and leaders of discipleship programs church-wide. If true discipleship is a process of transferring moral values and faith at the heart level, then an entirely different approach is needed. Our approach needs to include loving truth-telling and accountability about the way people are relating in their primary relationships so they can be drawn into the desired breakthroughs and growth in character that is fitting for Christ-followers. The church needs to rise to the challenge of becoming the place where people become free from the control and ravages of sin, and mature in love and Christlike character—a sanctified heart—making their family relationships whole. Unfortunately, the church as a whole has all but rejected the idea of relational accountability in its discipling practices. However, you have the power of God's grace within you to care about true spiritual growth, to realize and acknowledge that the heart-level quality of your relating habits and practices (as seen in your heart-level attitudes, intentions, and motivations) defines your morality and thus forms your character [the sum of your relating habits], reflecting your true spiritual condition and relationship with God.

We need a practical, working definition of morality that will impact the lives of average Christians who commonly serve the Lord in church settings. From now on, I hope that whenever you encounter the word "morality", you will remember to attach the clear and practical definition provided for you here—*Morality is the heart-level quality of how people relate with each other, defining character as the sum of our relational habits.* It's important to remember that the state of your relationships defines your character and reflects your true spiritual condition.

My Story ~ "At the Core"

When the Holy Spirit took me to the cross of death to my own selfish ways of relating and living, the process was fraught with inner turmoil, emotional upheaval, and uncertainty. The only thing I was certain of was that God Himself was leading me. I didn't know anything about what would await me. I just knew that He was God and that He was good. He patiently waited for me to come to the end of my own efforts to "save" myself, to "fix" my life, or otherwise "be in charge" of it. He waited for me to want nothing but Him, and when I finally gave myself up to His hand, He began accomplishing a powerful work in me at the core of my being.

I became a broken woman, and the Holy Spirit was released to live through me as I learned how to selflessly love others. While love became the spirit of my actions, God's wisdom began to increase for the changes I needed to make in my relating habits and patterns. I learned how to relate with the deep things going on inside of me, and the Holy Spirit's influence there.

> *"...The process was fraught with inner turmoil, emotional upheaval, and uncertainty. The only thing I was certain of was that God Himself was leading me...."*

I was profoundly amazed at the spiritual fruit the Lord began to give me and the peace of soul and affirmation I experienced from Him. God's work in my heart began to change the heartbeat of my family, and eventually, the moral culture of our home was transformed into a place where *Love* dwelled as our relationships became whole, reflecting the fruit of the Spirit in Christlike character. It's difficult to sum up whole-life change that transforms everything about who you've been. Here are only a few of the many changes in me and my family.

I went from not wanting my children around me to loving their presence in my daily life. I had been emotionally dependent upon my husband, Jim, and learned to have my deepest soul-felt needs met in the Lord, releasing him to his own growth process and making it possible for me to be a genuine help to him in it. I went from being helpless to address relational conflicts and misunderstandings to knowing how to help my children resolve theirs, and then as they matured I was so blessed to witness them practice reconciliation on their own. I had viewed motherhood as a thankless, unfulfilling burden from which I wanted an escape, but I became deeply grateful for the absolute joy and profound purpose it brought to my life. The Bible had been a mystery to me, but then the Holy Spirit brought it alive. And because holy love overflows and must find a landing place, life became filled with purpose, helping others come to that same love. God's glory is seen by His love in our lives.

A Merciful Reminder ~ *The state of your relationships defines your character and reflects your **true** spiritual condition. You are your children's character education.*

Testimonies

Tim and Barbie Poling describe how their children's behavior and forming character used to reflect who they were before God began to change their parenting practices.

> ***Tim*** ~ *My oldest daughter was harsh with the younger ones just like I was with all the kids. I had a problem with lying about things that would make me look bad, and my oldest son did that too. He had also begun to have angry outbursts toward his siblings. I was a perfectionist, and I refused to try anything or do anything that I couldn't do well or that might make me look bad. Several of my children were doing this too.*

> "My oldest daughter especially was beginning to hold her church friendships as much more valuable than her relationships within the family."
> ~ Barbie

> ***Barbie*** ~ *My children were definitely becoming who I was in the area of church service, friend focus, and using their talents to earn positions of ministry. I was doing the same. I thought I was serving God by doing these things. I wasn't conscious of how much I was actually using my talents and service to get attention and approval. I was very involved, and they were following right behind me. They found it very important to prove themselves to be dependable, responsible and faithful to*

the church leadership. My oldest daughter especially was beginning to hold her church friendships as much more valuable than her relationships within the family. As my children's talents became apparent, they delighted in being noticed and praised. At home, they were just like me in undisciplined messiness as well as in the way they relationally avoided and ignored their Grandma who lived with us as she needed our care and supervision.

8 Challenging Ideas and Corresponding Sobering Realities

Challenging Idea #1 *~ Most Christian parents don't know what moral and spiritual training consists of and are leaving it to chance.*

Sobering Reality #1 *~ You are being told on by your own relational fruit, but the hope is that God wants to empower you to change your fruit.*

Challenging Idea #2 *~ Morality is the heart-level quality of how people relate with each other, defining character as the sum of our relational habits.*

Sobering Reality #2 *~ The state of your relationships defines your character and reflects your true spiritual condition. You are your children's character education.*

Chapter 3

Instilling Moral Values at the Heart Level

~ Challenging Idea and Sobering Reality #3 ~
"It's impossible to transfer moral values in broad generalities that are unrelational. They are successfully instilled only by addressing the particulars of your family's heart-level relating habits and patterns."
~ A biblical morality is clearly defined in all of its relational particulars.

Now that we've taken a look at what morality is, let's look at how our own morality was formed. We likely have, as we parent, immorality at work in us through our particular relating patterns. When we can identify the *particulars* of our morality, we'll be able to understand what we may be transferring to our children.

A Void of Instruction

Each of us has probably engaged in a measure of self-examination if we're Christians saved by God's grace from our sins. However, if you went to school or were involved in church youth groups in the last thirty years, then chances are you were led to examine your morality only in *general* ways, such as lying, stealing, sleeping around, or doing drugs. In fact, shockingly so, you were probably actually encouraged to *independently* develop your own morality in all the particulars [how you treat your family and solve misunderstandings and conflict], according to how you *felt* about each *particular* situation.

This may be surprising, but as parental influence defaulted to the immature (children's peers and youth group leaders who are generally younger than the parents themselves), a void of true and much-needed relational instruction resulted, which led to much of the church actually embracing a *relative personal morality* along with the world and its educational system. This void has impacted us more than we know.

I want to give you a little history of how our secular culture and educational systems have addressed the notion of self-examination and introspection, which led to individuals forming their own personal morality apart from God. It is my hope you will begin to see how the church has been strongly and deeply influenced by secular culture's approach to addressing moral issues and why we are failing to instill moral character in our children.

> "The false idea was fostered that a person must have high self-esteem so he will choose to do good. He will be good simply because it feels better to be good."

A Cultural Rival ~ The Progressive Movement

According to James Davidson Hunter, author of *The Death of Character*, the progressive movement, which began a heavy influence at the beginning of the 20th century, sought to remove the notion of God's morality from the education of children. Their beliefs can be summed up so: *People naturally want to do good, because goodness comes from within the individual, and if they feel good enough about themselves, they will choose to do good.* They began the process of removing all references to God or religious sensibilities from instruction for children by exchanging words, such as "wrong" and "evil", for "unhealthy", "unsafe", and "unproductive." As their ideas for values clarification, and developing self-esteem gained ground, psychology became a dominant voice for deciding how morality should be passed on to children. Thus, the false idea was fostered that a person must have high self-esteem so he will choose to do good. He will be good simply because it feels better to be good.

> *"Common values are only self-evident in vague generalities."*

And so the thrust toward "morality" in schools is to help children feel good about themselves. This means that children are encouraged to make moral [relating] choices based upon what feels good to them and makes them feel better about themselves. The context of family and community, which has the ability to constrain and obligate individuals to moral behavior [quality relating habits], became irrelevant, leaving only the "self" as a reason for making moral [relational] decisions.

Self-Evident Common Values
~ Generalities or Particulars?

Psychologists say that if children are left alone to discover their true selves, they will automatically become morally good because common values are self-evident. But *common values are only self-evident in vague generalities.*

For instance, most people agree with the "general" idea that it's wrong to encroach upon their neighbor's physical property, which has well-defined boundaries. But not everyone agrees in the "particulars" of this value, for they may allow their dog to run free on their neighbor's property. Children who are not trained in the particulars of rightly relating grow up to become teenagers who see nothing wrong with being inconsiderate by disturbing the peace with their own loud music in a public park (encroaching upon another's sound space), or being pushy by tailgating to communicate impatience, or pushing into another's bodily space with unnecessary crowding while waiting in line at a store. Invisible and undetermined boundaries are where the *particulars* of the quality of morality come into play. There is a void of instruction in the particulars of relational circumstances, and so children by parental default are taught to do what feels good to them.

The core principle I want you to learn from this message is this: *It's impossible to transfer moral values in broad generalities that are unrelational. They are successfully instilled only by addressing the particulars of your family's heart-level relating habits and patterns.* It is not the general, but the particular, where values are actually transferred through a parent who cares about instilling such moral values in their children. A parent instructs in the particulars of any given situation.

For instance, in the above example of not encroaching on a neighbor's property, the parent might instruct, "Your music might be too loud for others who don't want to hear it; please be considerate and ask them if they mind." Or when standing in a checkout line, "Stand back and give people a little personal space." These relational instructions (and many that are more serious) are not contained in the generally agreed-upon morality of "Don't lie, steal, or murder." A relative particular morality, brought on by children not being with parents often enough who provide loving instruction, actually blurs the lines between what is right and what is wrong, resulting in a society where morality [the quality of how people relate with each other] continues to be on a steady decline.

Agreed Upon Character Qualities

Fast forward to the 1980s when there was an outcry of sorts against what had come to be known as values-clarification. Parents wanted a return to teaching right and wrong in the schools. As a result, a curriculum was formed generally called "Character Education" (CE). An agreed-upon list of good character qualities that have been taught throughout history in many different cultures was gathered, and strategies were developed for teaching them to children. However, the self-centered focus remained the same: *we should be good because it makes us feel good, and if you like yourself enough, you will choose to do good.* This emphasis was the only option for approaching so-called character development because the agreed-upon qualities were necessarily limited to only those *everyone* could agree upon, and not all people agree that God's Moral Law of Love is the standard for character. Thus, in the desire not to offend anyone and to be inclusive, we now have the *death of character*.

The Spread of Relative Morality, and thus, Error

The idea that if you like yourself enough you will choose to do good is the same underlying assumption that eventually became the basis for other programs in non-educational institutions that are attempting to teach character to young people. A few such institutions are the YMCA, scouting clubs, anti-drug programs, and even abstinence programs. You may be thinking that the church is doing better than this, right?

Unfortunately, the church has been deeply influenced by the spread of relative morality. This influence eventually affected how young Christians were discipled church-wide to the point where, research shows, "sin" is rarely ever mentioned. There doesn't seem to be a program that actually addresses God's moral standards—in all of its particulars—as the reason for doing and being good. If a person feels uneasy due to conviction, the common response is to project on the source of said conviction, because after all, it's been instilled in them that they're supposed to feel good about themselves—and conviction of wrong doesn't feel good.

As Charles Colson observed, the conscience has been exchanged for a "barometer of our emotional state" instead of having a strong internal monitor of moral [relational] choices. These observations point back to the influence of the progressive movement in the public schools, which apparently has influenced the church as well, turning us away from truth and leading us into error.

A Common Approach to Discipleship

A common approach to working with young people, both among Christian youth leaders and even some Christian counselors, is to help them realize how much God loves them; to view God as a loving Father, compassionate, merciful, and generous. These are important aspects to communicate about God's character. However, leaders leave out the part about His parenting practices that bring daily correction and instruction to our relationships through disciplinary processes to form us into the character of His Son. Instead, they think that simply knowing God loves them is supposed to make people feel better about themselves as "adopted children of God." A well-known Christian child psychologist conveys to young people that all they need for a sense of moral well-being are a "sustained introspective gaze and self-understanding." Developing a conceptual understanding of their identity in Christ is supposed to give them healthier self-esteem, and somehow lead them to stop sinning. Sermons and messages preached from pulpits across America utilize this same approach.

> *"The false discipleship approach of developing a conceptual identity takes people around their conscience— preventing them from making a true connection with God and others."*

There is a problem with this approach in connection to how people relate with each other. It circumvents the true conscience, providing only an informational learning experience about God and who they are in Christ that doesn't have the hope of bringing the person any closer to actually knowing God or truly feeling better about themselves. Providing only information *about* God denies the power of God for salvation and inner change that would bring a person's true identity into reality and provide a true motivation for doing good, and the enabling power to carry out God's will. The false discipleship approach of developing only a conceptual identity takes people around their conscience—preventing them from making a truthful connection with God and others.

Religious Research

The research backs this up. Hunter of *The Death of Character,* found some disturbing evidence in a representative sample of children across the country with various religious backgrounds. More than 53% of the children and teens would make moral decisions based upon what they themselves deem to be best. These children would choose what is best for their peer community (humanists, 20%); what improves their personal situation the best (utilitarians, 10%); or makes them feel the best (expressivists, 18%). Of the remaining 47% of the children, 20% said they would do what their parents or teachers said to do (conventionalists), and only 16% said they would do what the Bible said to do (theists).

The study goes on to show that the students in the combination group (of humanists, utilitarians, and expressivists), in responding to various given situations, would make significantly more immoral and unloving decisions than the other two groups. The common self-esteem teaching in schools and in churches that is meant to improve character actually produces people who are more immoral [unloving]. And of course, the results in much of today's churched youth are self-evident.

This historical review is to point out that our secular culture knows the need for character, but they want to do the right thing in the wrong way, keeping self-centeredness unchallenged. Secular culture has the same claims as the truth, but it's in competition *against* God. Man's approach actually *erodes* character and morality.

The Scriptures say, *"For my thoughts are not your thoughts, neither are your ways my ways, saith the LORD"* (Isaiah 55:8). God has a plan for connecting with Him, for our well-being, and for how to know His love and goodness and our identity as His child. Merely acquiring intellectual knowledge of Him, and mentally convincing ourselves He is good and He loves us, will not accomplish much—but maybe a lifetime of spiritual frustration.

The Way Morality Is Formed

Moral Character [Christlike relating habits] is necessary for a family to hold together. When families fall apart or fester in dysfunction, it is always due to the moral culture of the home. Teenage independence, resistance or rebellion, sibling conflicts, spouses at odds with each other, "personality conflicts", distance, and independent living—these are all signs of dysfunction due to the heartbeat of the family relationships being neglected. The school and church cannot be held responsible simply because they are not the ones who have been tasked with forming Christlike character in children. Parents are the ones assigned by God to instill moral character in their children.

In order to be available to God for a work of righteousness in our lives, we need to come to understand how moral character is formed. Most people agree that the way to improve the character of a culture is to start with the young. If most children learn good character before they become adults, then the culture as a whole will become more moral [relationally functional]. Since our culture feels the need to pass on character to children, and since most children go to school, the schools believe they have the main responsibility for the job. The church tends to possess this same attitude of "ownership" toward children.

However, we've already seen how the schools can only address morality in general ways leaving most moral [relational] decisions up to children to make on their own. The schools can teach not to steal and not to be violent, but they can't teach how to serve with a good attitude or how to keep from being manipulative. They can't address self-seeking thought processes, such as perfectionism, self-justification, denial, criticalness, complaining, or emotional manipulation. They can't address controlling behaviors, wrong motivations in relationships, or wrong attitudes and intentions that fuel unhealthy relating practices.

As Christians, we know it is not the government's place to form character, but it is given to the church to care about developing a well-defined moral standard that is based upon Christ's Law of Love—God's relational value system.

Parents need encouragement from their church to be responsible in the forming of their children's character, and any programs the family is involved with at church ought to support and uphold the complete responsibility and authority of parents in this holy endeavor.

Personal Story ~ "What A Mess!"

I was raised in the Catholic Church and educated by nuns in Catholic schools. I am deeply fond of my Catholic roots and enjoyed many aspects of my religious upbringing. However, my training was superficial in that it only provided me with a *general* morality. Being good meant obeying my parents, doing the right things by going to church daily on the way to school and every Sunday, confession once a month, and participating in all the religious disciplines of the church calendar. I stopped going to church when I graduated high school and left home, which meant to me that I no longer met the requirements for being good and righteous. I operated in a strong relative personal morality that was fueled by the "new" moral freedoms of the 1960s. "I'm okay, you're okay" and "whatever makes you feel good" became a couple of my mottos, and so if I felt like doing something, I just did it with no concern for how it affected others. Actually, I was clueless that my behavior and decisions had any effect whatsoever on anyone else.

> *"Actually, I was clueless that my behavior and decisions had any effect whatsoever on anyone else."*

As a result, when I returned to church at the age of twenty-six, I picked up religious activity where I left off, becoming *generally* moral once again. It wasn't until I was thirty-three in April of 1984 when I was born again by God's grace that I came to see I was really a very immoral person. The poor fruit of my *particular* morality was born out of years of self-centered, dysfunctional relating. For the first time in my life, I saw my life for what it was, and it was a mess! I began to allow God to do a work in me, by repositioning my life to be available to Him.

This is when I began to experiment with parenting approaches, but because I didn't understand what it was God was after in me, it would be another three years before I allowed Him to have complete access to my heart [my conscience, attitudes, intentions, and motivations]. I surrendered as fully as I knew how and the fruit of my relationships began to change.

It is my dearest hope you will have the benefit of some understanding through these messages so you can cooperate with God more quickly, and the work needed in your life can be accomplished more efficiently. Don't waste another moment. Trust the Holy Spirit to lead you to full surrender, allowing God to work in your heart toward making the needed changes in your relating habits and patterns.

A Merciful Reminder ~ A biblical morality is clearly defined in all of its relational particulars.

Testimonies

Tim describes his *general* morality and how it was formed in him, making him a "good" person, and the fruit it produced in his life—his *appearance* of righteousness.

> *I followed the outward behavior rules that my parents taught me. I was sitting down on the outside, but standing up on the inside. I was supposed to go to church, read my Bible, and pray. I wasn't supposed to smoke or drink or sleep around. I obeyed the laws of society and thought of myself as a good citizen. I believed the traditional values that it was my duty as a husband to work at my job and provide material things for my family while my wife did her duty of caring for the house and children. I believed I was a good person because I was responsible with my money.*

> "I followed the outward behavior rules that my parents taught me. I was sitting down on the outside, but standing up on the inside." ~ Tim

> *My "general" morality led me to believe that as a good Christian I should be involved in the church, and give money and time toward church efforts. I was proud of the money I gave, and I was overly concerned that the church met my expectation for using it wisely. I felt the church should be extra grateful for my service. I became a leader in the church while being easily frustrated with and critical of other volunteers. I advanced in*

my career at work and this made me feel righteous because as the legalistic master of my family, I was providing for them, and I was very proud of my work. I made sure I wasn't an offensive person by being extra careful not to upset people. I thought of myself as dependable and trustworthy and I was critical of those who I thought were not. My general sense of what was right and wrong led me to lie about and hide those areas of my life where I was not obeying the don'ts of my outward behavioral rules. Because I felt that being responsible with money made me righteous, I would regularly get very angry with my wife over how we spent money.

Tim describes his previous discipleship in the particulars of his morality—how he was taught or what he caught by way of relating to the people in his life.

My attitudes, motivations, and ways of relating were not addressed by my parents. I did the minimum amount of following the rules of my general morality so I could say I was doing it. I learned from my environment that it was just fine to make other people feel stupid so that I could build myself up. I also learned to blame others for anything that happened, and to be critical and self-righteously disgusted with people. I learned to be proud and arrogant.

My "particular" relational fruit was self-righteous and judgmental. I was harshly critical of others who didn't share my outward behavioral rules. I actually believed myself to be superior because of my education and my appearance of righteousness. This led me to feel justified in blaming my wife for any situation that I thought made me look bad. If the house wasn't picked up and dinner wasn't on time when I got home, my arrogance led me to assume that my wife wasn't fulfilling her duty. I believed I had done my part by getting up early and going to work so I showered her with displeasure and often anger. If the kids were noisy or didn't do exactly what I wanted, I would get frustrated with them and treated them harshly by speaking sternly with anger and physically handling them roughly. I often didn't communicate what I wanted, but I expected them to know what I wanted.

> *"I was left to myself to establish my thought processes and attitudes."*
> *~ Barbie*

Barbie describes her *general* morality and how it was formed in her, making her a "good" person, and the fruit it produced in her life—her a*ppearance* of righteousness.

> *The "general" morality learned from my family and Christian school consisted of several big do's and don'ts. I didn't smoke or drink or sleep around. I went to church, studied the Bible, and I was determined to date only Christians and marry a Christian man, and listen to only Christian music. Later in my life, I adopted more do's and don'ts. I would homeschool, have regular devotional times, and I would be involved in church programs.*
>
> *My "general" morality led me to surround myself with people who held the same set of do's and don'ts as I did, and it led me to teach my children the same. As I allowed the Lord to expose to me my self-centeredness, I began to see that I was arrogant in believing that my morality was exemplary and that others needed to strive to become more like me. Since I thought of myself as being a very obedient believer, I subconsciously thought that others would need to become more like me in their do's and*

don'ts if they were to become obedient believers too. My general morality also produced in me the belief that I didn't have much to repent for. I knew that the Bible said that all had sinned so I mentally believed I was a sinner, but I couldn't really think of what I was doing to sin.

Barbie describes her previous discipleship in the particulars of her morality—how she was taught or what she caught by way of relating to the people in her life.

I don't recall ever having had my attitudes, motivations or thoughts addressed by my parents or any other adults in my life. I had a great deal of bad attitudes and unkind behavior both at home and at school that were never discussed or addressed in any way. I bore the brunt of bad attitudes and unkind relating from neighbor kids and kids at school, as well as from siblings. I never talked with my parents or anyone about these things. I was left to myself to figure out how to relate and how to deal with conflict, hurts and wounds. My overall relational pattern became one of expecting people to reject me and surrounding myself with people who seemed to be impressed by me. I manipulated circumstances so I could keep the favor of people I wanted to please. These "particular" relational habits produced a strong desire to be controlled by those in my life from whom I wanted approval. I was easily controlled by people in leadership positions. Over time, I would work my mind trying to figure out how to do things just the way they would like. This led me to commit myself to obligations of church service which negatively impacted my family. I was also controlled by my husband. I worked very hard to manipulate circumstances to keep him from getting angry with me. I would rush around trying to make things just right before he got home. I was never successful at keeping him from being angry so I would take on blame and apologize for things I didn't do, trying to restore peace and the feeling that I had his approval back again. Toward my children, I was more controlling. I was sometimes overly stern or harsh and I showered them with a general sense of disapproval for their subtle resistance toward me. In relating to my friends, I subtly paraded my talents in order to impress them. I later realized that I was really just using them to get approval and praise for myself. It seemed like this made me feel better about myself.

Barbie describes how her attitudes, motivations, and thought processes were shaped and formed through her upbringing.

I know that my motivation toward approval-seeking was formed in me by the neglect I experienced from the adults in my life. My need to be known, understood, and directed in my attitudes, motivations and thought processes was not met. I was left to myself to establish my thought processes and attitudes. Because I suffered rejection both at home and at school, my motivations were turned toward finding approval and acceptance for myself. I felt like I found it at Christian school in showing how much biblical knowledge I had and how much I could attain. I also found it in being a "servant" in church activities. I had abilities that were desirable in church programs, and it seemed like my participation brought me the kind of praise and approval that I wanted.

There were a couple of kids in my childhood who used angry rejection and sulking to get the people around them to give attention and concern. I really looked up to these kids and wanted their favor. Through my interactions with them, I became fearful that their angry rejection would be turned toward me. I was motivated to fix things or modify my behavior in order to escape the possibility of being the object of their anger and rejection. I had no one in my life who knew of my thoughts and fears or would give me guidance in developing different relational habits. My flesh was in charge of my relational character formation.

> "I don't recall ever having had my attitudes, motivations, or thoughts addressed by my parents or any other adults in my life. I had a great deal of bad attitudes and unkind behavior both at home and at school that were never discussed or addressed in any way." ~ Barbie

8 Challenging Ideas and Corresponding Sobering Realities

Challenging Idea #1 ~ *Most Christian parents don't know what moral and spiritual training consists of and are leaving it to chance.*

Sobering Reality #1 ~ *You are being told on by your own relational fruit, but the hope is that God wants to empower you to change your fruit.*

Challenging Idea #2 ~ *Morality is the heart-level quality of how people relate with each other, defining character as the sum of our relational habits.*

Sobering Reality #2 ~ *The state of your relationships defines your character and reflects your true spiritual condition. You are your children's character education.*

Challenging Idea #3 ~ *It's impossible to transfer moral values in broad generalities that are unrelational. They are successfully instilled only by addressing the particulars of your family's heart-level relating habits and patterns.*

Sobering Reality #3 ~ *A biblical morality is clearly defined in all of its relational particulars.*

Chapter 4

Our Purpose ~ Learning to Love Much and Well

~ Challenging Idea and Sobering Reality #4 ~
"True spiritual growth occurs when we bring our particular morality in line with Christ's Law of Love, making our instruction in moral rectitude completely relational."
~ Love's evidence [God's standard for moral fruit] is seen in the sacrificial quality of the heart-level attitudes, intentions, and motivations of your relating practices.

It's not surprising, when confronted by our own immorality, that some of us would automatically assume that we need to increase our spiritual activity or religious duties to "get closer to God" so we can overcome. Some might pursue more intellectual accumulation of Bible knowledge in an attempt to learn some trick to defeating sin. Others might need to "feel better" about themselves, and so read material that encourages them about their identity in Christ to lift their self-esteem. Some will blame it all on an attack from the devil. Some surround themselves with spiritual talk and with others who engage in spiritual talk. However, if our hearts are not right with God, none of these religious activities will provide the spiritual breakthroughs we need. As is often the case, they will keep us sidetracked from what God wants to do, and worse yet anesthetize us from experiencing our true need. We need a change of focus, making our purpose LOVE. When we begin to address the particulars of our relating patterns, our parenting practices will change and we'll be able to instill true biblical morality in our children. Let's take a look at what our particular morality is supposed to look like and what we are supposed to be transferring to our children.

Common Discipleship Models Don't Provide Believers with a Relational Context

Unfortunately, the church, in general, has fostered the notion of independence by having fully embraced the false ideas of the progressive movement that produce relative personal morality. Each one goes his own way, forming his own ideas for spiritual growth with little to no actual accountability to known moral standards within their family relationships or church community. Examples might include: acquiring Bible knowledge, doing good works, and engaging in spiritual disciplines that are divorced from reality or being involved in various spiritual activities or "movements."

> *"We must come to learn how to love and develop Christlike character that results in a higher quality of moral and spiritual rectitude."*

Morality is formed and expressed only in relationships. True biblical spirituality can only be expressed there as well. Here is what I want you to take from this message:

True spiritual growth occurs when we bring our particular morality in line with Christ's Law of Love, making our instruction in moral rectitude completely relational. By removing spiritual discipleship from morality's relational context—removing it from reality—the church has sabotaged its own efforts to be an influence of light in a darkened culture and robbed following generations of a personally enriching spiritual legacy.

We must learn how to disciple and instruct people, including children, within a relational context. We must begin to address relational habits and patterns of behavior that affect the well-being of family relationships. *We must come to learn how to love and develop Christlike character that results in a higher quality of moral and spiritual rectitude.* Remember that moral and spiritual rectitude is about the *quality of love* in our relationships.

The New Testament is full of references to Christ's kind of love. The Apostles Paul, Peter, and John continually exhorted the church to learn how to love. It is spelled out clearly and specifically in their letters to the churches. Love is the focus. Love is the goal. And Love is the purpose of the Christian life. There are however pitfalls to understanding Love's focus, goals, and purpose.

Pitfalls to Understanding Love's Focus, Goals, and Purpose

One common assumption I've seen people make is that if they are basically respectful and are not intentionally being socially offensive to one another, minding their own business so to speak, then they think they are walking in love. In the *Six Megathemes Emerge* from research conducted by the Barna Group for 2010, Barna points to the idea that love has been redefined to mean *"the absence of conflict and confrontation as though there are no moral absolutes that are worth fighting for."* Some believe that if they participate in church service by helping out, then they are walking in sacrificial love. This is not so. Developing sacrificial qualities of love, and therefore moral rectitude, requires much intentional action toward understanding one another in our close relationships. Paul exhorts us to learn to love well.

> *"So this is my prayer: that your love will flourish and that you will not only love much but well."*
>
> Philippians 1:9 The Message

Learning to Love Well ~ Common Christian Teachings Don't Provide Believers with Such Instruction

Paul qualifies the *quality* of our behavior with others under our charge or in the sphere of our relational influence. He tells us to love *much* and love *well*. Examining the following passage can be quite sobering given the mixed personal agendas that get in the way of simply treating one another with love, especially our own children if we want to influence them for Christ.

> *"The whole point of what we're urging is simply love—love uncontaminated by self-interest and counterfeit faith, a life open to God. Those who fail to keep to this point soon wander off into cul-de-sacs of gossip. They set themselves up as experts on religious issues, but haven't the remotest idea of what they're holding forth with such imposing eloquence. It's true that moral guidance and counsel need to be given, but the way you say it and to whom you say it are as important as what you say..."*
>
> 1 Timothy 1:5-6 The Message

If the whole point of all of our interactions is love, uncontaminated by self-interests, placing true love in the realm of self-sacrifice in relationships—then why are we not as individuals and as the church focusing on the weightier matters of healing family relationships and forming particular moral character? These purposes require self-sacrifice in relationships. Self-sacrifice is usually equated with church service, teaching Sunday School, cleaning the church, and other such volunteer activities. However, many Christians who volunteer still possess obviously broken relationships that never get addressed in their spiritual growth. Are we so failing to see this contradiction between the two—the command to love while at the same time allowing our relationships to go unhealed?

In order to walk as a true believer, our righteousness must exude LOVE, and the *intentional pursuit of mending and healing broken relationships.* Healing our relationships in the Lord and making them whole IS the path to developing moral character and thus enabling true spiritual growth. There is no other way. When we avoid or otherwise accept as "normal" our various relational dysfunctions, we sabotage every other effort toward true spiritual growth, keeping us in a state of guilt and confusion. Scripturally sound spirituality grows a real person and an authentic Christian who can love much and love well.

Without love, Paul demonstrates how Christians try to compensate with all sorts of wicked activity to make themselves feel important, and to cover up their lack of God's love in their lives. Under the pretense of caring for others, they gossip, and under the pretense of spiritual growth, they become so-called experts on religious or biblical issues. There is no compensation for lack of love—nothing can replace it. When we don't love, especially in our families, others miss out on knowing Christ through us. They miss out on experiencing healing love that can only come through human agency. Love is the enabling force for good works. A void of love in people's primary relationships is what prevents them from truly serving, caring, giving, and reaching out to others in need. Paul's prayers for the saints were always about love.

The Activity of Developing Moral Character through Loving Relationships

> *"And this I pray: that your love may abound yet more and more and extend to its fullest development in knowledge and all keen insight [that your love may display itself in greater depth of acquaintance and more comprehensive discernment]."*
>
> Philippians 1:9-11 AMP

What a goal—to fully develop our love! And Paul qualifies how the activity of developing our love is supposed to look. Again, it's the *quality* of our love, and the extent to which we are to go to invest in knowing each other, proving our love—*"...in knowledge and all keen insight and greater depth of acquaintance and more comprehensive discernment."* I hope this shines more light on Jesus' two commandments—*"You shall love the Lord your God with all your heart and with all your soul and with all your mind (intellect)...You shall love your neighbor as [you do] yourself."* In other words, you shall abound in love toward each other, and develop your love fully in knowledge and all keen insight of each other, starting in your family.

Love Abounding

Love abounding in the knowledge of God and of others requires that we actually know God and those we love. What you are attracted to, you will grow in the knowledge of, and soon come to love the object of your attraction. If you are attracted to birds or insects, you will seek to grow in the knowledge of birds and insects. If you love cats, dogs or horses, you will seek to grow in the knowledge of how to relate with them. Likewise, if you love your children, you will seek to grow in the knowledge of who they are as God made them. Their true identity includes their inborn "unique creative profile" of gifts, talents, abilities, interests, bents, and peculiar motivations. Love will bring you to a deep desire to know them for who they really are instead of expecting them to conform to your prescribed image of what you think they should be. Your instruction toward them will begin to reflect the fact that you are coming to know and understand them deeply, and thus loving them. This demands an intimate relationship where hearts are fully locked together in mutual trust.

Being involved in discipleship groups, home groups, worship team, and other such activities lead believers to think they are "loving others" when they respond to others in their fellowship by offering prayer or a listening ear. In reality, very few believers possess the spiritual maturity and character [the love] necessary to actually walk a path with a hurting person, helping them to successfully address the problems in their life. If you haven't learned how to do this with your own children you certainly won't be able to help anyone else.

Let's break down how Paul instructs us to love one another. Instead of viewing the following ideas in the context of church-type activities, will you read them taking into consideration the relationships in your own family, between spouses, between parents and children, and between siblings? The family is where it all begins.

- That love abounds more and more toward each other.

- That love extends to its fullest development of each other.

- That love develops with knowledge of each other.

- That love develops with keen insight of each other.

- That love displays in greater depth of acquaintance of each other [familiar and intimate knowledge of].

- That love develops with more comprehensive discernment of each other.

- That love comes to understand each other as fully as is humanly possible.

The family certainly has a lot of work to do! With a focus on this one objective—learning how to Love, the family can set goals for Christlike character formation, and develop more meaningful purpose that can influence all of their shared and independent activities. The growth process of learning to love well provides the instruction that prevents the forming of damaging judgments, harmful assumptions, and jumping to conclusions that cause us to take actions either away from or against others. When we display our love through a greater depth of acquaintance [familiar and intimate knowledge of] and more comprehensive discernment, we come to fully understand each other. Wow!

My Story ~ "Becoming Real ~ The Velveteen Rabbit"

Remember *The Velveteen Rabbit*—the story of the stuffed toy a boy loved so much it became real. In a true sense, this is what happens when we experience God's love enough to break through the barriers we've erected to keep people out, forcing them to relate with our false personality [our habitual unloving relational patterns]. When barriers come down we become real people, able to love others and touch their hearts. The parental love I had for my first son was no less than what I had for my other children, but it didn't reach his heart and had no power to change him while he was growing up. Whereas, after the Lord changed me, my parental love—influenced by God's love in me—enabled me to meet my younger children's soul-felt needs so they not only *intellectually* knew I loved them, but they *experienced* my love daily. Furthermore, I was empowered to help them become aware of their emotional nature and the inner workings of their own hearts, and thus help them change from the inside out, forming Christlike character. True sacrificial qualities of love, while relating at the heart level, effectively dealt a death blow to self-centeredness and brought our relationships into the place of reality. We became spiritually aware and alive.

> *"I entered into a tangible spiritual significance of being in the center of God's activity, where love is, where His focus is, where His best work is, and where vital purpose is."*

Becoming real began by simply allowing God to tell me the truth and agreeing with Him. I had been a mere shell of a real person, bereft of love and void of the Spirit. But when I allowed Jesus to break through my defenses, He changed me and filled me with His love. I became alive unto God and present to Him and His purposes in my home. Becoming real was like leaving a detached place where I had been a mere spectator of life. I entered into a tangible spiritual significance of being in the center of God's activity, where love is, where His focus is, where His best work is, and where vital purpose is. Becoming real enabled me to communicate at the heart level with others and help them overcome their sin and carnal relating patterns, leading to healing in their relationships. Becoming real led me to give out what had so generously been given to me. Becoming real made me an *authentic* Christian.

What a Goal!

Our morality is supposed to be that of loving well. To flourish and grow in our love for one another is to love well. To be in true grace toward others is to love well. To mix our faith in with our love, trusting God to give us keen insight, greater depth of acquaintance, and more comprehensive discernment toward those under our charge is to love well. To speak truth, and even say hard things with loving understanding, is to love well. To seek to guide, lead, and instruct others according to the Spirit's wisdom instead of according to our own worldly and fleshly ways is to love well. Loving well is possessing spiritual and moral rectitude and true righteousness. My! What a goal! How do we learn to love well?

Establishing a Relational Parenting Model

The principle of relationship—life's most central lesson—silently influences our entire life whether for good or for evil. We are either building and strengthening our relationships through loving relational practices or we are tearing them apart with our unloving habits and patterns. We need healthy relationships for any spiritual growth effort or transfer of moral rectitude to be fruitful. Leading our children to the ways of the Lord requires close, loving, heart-level relationships that are building and growing stronger. Our morality is expressed and experienced in the way we relate with our family. We are our children's moral models, and the way we relate with them automatically instills in them the quality of our own morality. We need to challenge our moral character to reflect Christ's character by learning to love much and love well. We need to examine and change our own relating patterns.

To establish a relational parenting model, we become hard-pressed to understand God's relational standards and His Moral Law, which leads us to allow Him to parent us first. Through right relating with Him, we come to know Him and His ways. Standards expose our shortcomings and give us something concrete to aim for. Since God's standards are overshadowed by the world's standards, we really do need the Word of God to shed light in our darkened, personal world if we are to become truly righteous. There are many love commands given in Scripture, providing instruction for how to love (see the companion volume to this book, *Love's Character Qualities Companion Tool*) to get you started on a path of understanding this profound and potentially life-changing exhortation to the church.

My Story ~ "Course Corrections"

During my first three and a half years as a Christian believer, I tried to do the "right things" based on church assumptions. I plunged myself into church activity. There wasn't much of a homeschool community at that time; it was still forming underground, but when I began to go around homeschoolers, it was easy to see that they adopted a mixture of ideas, some of which I came to see often contradicted the Gospel they believed in. This caused a bit of uncertainty in me at that time, but I trusted the Holy Spirit's course corrections whenever I started to stray toward false teachings or simply mix with other emphases, which when followed would have prevented me from apprehending His life more fully. The Lord kept me focused on His narrow path toward manifesting more and more Life and Love. God certainly knows how to lead if we will choose to follow Him, leaving behind other influences.

A Single Approach to Moral Rectitude and True Spiritual Growth

There is only one approach to spiritual growth that empowers relationships and causes emotional maturity: develop true moral rectitude at the heart level, forming Christlike character. I'm going to say it several more times with different expressions.

- *One cannot develop their moral character [the quality and sum of relating habits] without addressing how they relate with those people who are the closest to them. This means that when you agree to wrong relating practices with your spouse, you are acting immorally, and not being a true helper to your spouse. Relational moral character is very particular.*

- *In other words, one cannot develop Christlike moral character and grow up spiritually outside the context of addressing their personal relationships with the aid of the Holy Spirit's influence on the conscience and obedience in truth-telling. This means that merely engaging in individual or corporate spiritual activity does not make one mature. Instilling Christlike moral character is a process of many particular awakenings to conscience that lead to many positive actions of change.*

Dallas Willard, in Renovation of the Heart, puts it well:

"Spiritual formation, good or bad, is always profoundly social. You cannot keep it to yourself. Anyone who thinks of it as a merely private matter has misunderstood it. Anyone who says, 'It's just between me and God,' or 'What I do is my own business,' has misunderstood God… Strictly speaking there is nothing 'just between me and God.' For all that is between me and God affects who I am; and that, in turn, modifies my relationship to everyone around me. My relationship to others also modifies me and deeply affects my relationship to God. Hence those relationships must be transformed if I am to be transformed."

- *I'll say it again, there is no such thing as morality [moral rectitude—true spiritual growth and maturity] apart from learning how to relate correctly in Christlike love.*

- *Spiritual growth that is scripturally sound [moral character-formation toward Christlikeness] always leads to an ability to love selflessly. This means that much of the "spiritual growth" emphasis delivered through the teachings and preaching in America's churches is biblically unfruitful.*

- *Working in association with a church ministry, while allowing your broken relationships to go unmended, is not a substitute for spiritual maturity or moral character, and is in no way an indication you are in right standing with God.*

- *And again, true spiritual growth and maturity are impossible while remaining emotionally immature. This means you could be pretending.*

- *Emotional immaturity is immoral because it is self-centered and unloving.*

- *Emotional and spiritual maturity are inseparable.*

- *Relational maturity and moral rectitude are inseparable. You are the only one who is being fooled by your imbalanced emotional nature.*

- *True godliness is moral rectitude, and it exhibits qualities of Christlike love, which is always sacrificial in the attitudes, intents, and motives of the heart, and it produces intimate heart bonds.*

- *Godliness is not determined by being turned toward spiritual activities and Bible studies.*

- *Our human relations directly reflect how we are really relating with God, and communicate to any onlooker what kind of Christian we really are, and what moral values we really have.*

- *If our relationships are growing stronger and deeper then we are growing spiritually, rising in moral rectitude.*

- *All true spiritual growth addresses and solves life's relational problems.*

- *There is no such thing as our "spiritual life" and then our "real life" or our "family life"; it is all one.*

- *The true quality and condition of our internal spiritual life can be tested by examining our external relational fruit.*

- *True morality and Christlike character exist only at the heart level—the seat of conscience where all relating habits and patterns are formed.*

- *Our current moral condition is determined by how we relate with our inner driving force—our conscience.*

As professional counselors, Drs. Cloud and Townsend of How People Grow, began searching for what seemed to be a missing key to true spiritual growth. They asked, *"How could there be spiritual growth and then other growth?"* They—like Jesus—believed that all of life is spiritual and that God is involved in every area of life. They believed that spiritual growth should be influencing the functional areas of life as well as the spiritual ones. They asked, *"How does spiritual growth address and solve life's problems?"* Here is what happened:

> *"I saw that everything I had been learning that helped people grow was right there in the Bible all along. All of the processes that had changed peoples' lives were in the pages of Scripture. The Bible talked about the things that helped people grow in*

relational and emotional areas as well as spiritual ones. I was ecstatic. Not only was the Bible true, but also what was true was in the Bible!...

"First, when people came to us for counseling, we wanted them to understand that the issues they were working on were not growth issues or counseling issues, but spiritual growth issues. Spiritual growth, in our mind, was the answer to everything. Second, we wanted to bring the idea of working on relational and emotional issues back into the mainstream of spiritual growth. Spiritual growth should affect relationship problems, emotional problems, and all other problems of life. There is no such thing as our 'spiritual life' and then our 'real life.' It is all one."

They set about to link the spiritual and the practical with a scriptural understanding of how growth takes place. This is also the purpose of the ministry, *Empowering Hearts Ministry*, to demonstrate how scriptural inner growth takes place, resulting in moral rectitude and true spiritual growth and whole relationships.

A Merciful Reminder ~ *Love's evidence [God's standard for moral fruit] is seen in the sacrificial quality of the heart-level attitudes, intentions, and motivations of your relating practices.*

> "Our human relations directly reflect how we are really relating with God, and communicate to any onlooker what kind of Christian we really are."

Testimonies

Barbie describes some of the relational changes in her family since she began to learn what real love looks like and to practice loving well.

> ***My 13-yr-old son*** *I came to understand that my children needed me to pour affection, understanding, and encouragement on them, as well as very basic regular instruction in order for them to be able to obey and to learn to love their siblings and the Lord from their hearts. My oldest son's heart, in particular, was very distant from me by the time he was thirteen. As I began to lavish affection and approval on him, encouraging him in the small disciplines of his life, he came to a point of confessing his hidden sin to me. He then made an abrupt shift in his heart toward me and toward the Lord in obeying his conscience. He earnestly pursued loving his siblings in very practical ways and thirsting for my instruction and counsel in all areas of his life.*
>
> ***My 14-yr-old daughter*** *Through this change in my son, I became more aware of the distance of heart in my oldest daughter who was then fourteen. Her heart was easily drawn toward me and toward the Lord as I poured on the affection and approval that she needed.*
>
> ***My younger children*** *I had not yet lost the hearts of my younger children, and now I know I never will. Previously, my children merely got along without much unkindness or outburst, but in a short time, they came to thoroughly enjoy each other's company, being eagerly interested in each other and their interests and willingly and generously helping and supporting one another in all their endeavors.*

My husband *The most extensive change was in my relationship with my husband. I stopped trying to protect myself from my husband's anger. I stopped rushing around trying to fix things when he was angry, and instead told him he was wrong to be angry. I stopped receiving blame from him and instead I told him he was wrong to blame me. I repented to him for enabling him to treat us badly and for loving myself while leaving him trapped in his sin. I prayed for him to become free, and the Lord gave me a great deal of revelation for him, helping him to understand his sinful patterns. The huge change in his heart and the resulting change in his behavior brought radical change in our entire family dynamic.*

8 Challenging Ideas and Corresponding Sobering Realities

Challenging Idea #1 *~ Most Christian parents don't know what moral and spiritual training consists of and are leaving it to chance.*

Sobering Reality #1 *~ You are being told on by your own relational fruit, but the hope is that God wants to empower you to change your fruit.*

Challenging Idea #2 *~ Morality is the heart-level quality of how people relate with each other, defining character as the sum of our relational habits.*

Sobering Reality #2 *~ The state of your relationships defines your character and reflects your true spiritual condition. You are your children's character education.*

Challenging Idea #3 *~ It's impossible to transfer moral values in broad generalities that are unrelational. They are successfully instilled only by addressing the particulars of your family's heart-level relating habits and patterns.*

Sobering Reality #3 *~ A biblical morality is clearly defined in all of its relational particulars.*

Challenging Idea #4 ~ *True spiritual growth occurs when we bring our particular morality in line with Christ's Law of Love, making our instruction in moral rectitude completely relational.*

Sobering Reality #4 ~ *Love's evidence [God's standard for moral fruit] is seen in the sacrificial quality of the heart-level attitudes, intentions, and motivations of your relating practices.*

Chapter 5

Calling Relational Immorality What It Is ~ Sin

~ Challenging Idea and Sobering Reality #5 ~
*"Relational immorality is sin, and sin—simply stated—
is a self-centered failure to love, and falling short of
love is immoral in God's eyes, even wicked and evil."
~ Heart attitudes, intentions, and motivations toward others
tell the truth about the quality of your morality.*

The Law of Liberty

How do we learn to love well? The apostles and Christ's disciples were in constant remembrance that the New Moral Law of Love was the focus, goal, and purpose of the Christian life. They knew this because they had been released—liberated by the indwelling Holy Spirit—from the Old Testament requirements of the Law. They were now free to simply LOVE.

What they experienced came to be known as the Law of Liberty (James 1:25).

The Law of Liberty is a principle comprehensive of all the Scriptures. It is not a law of compulsion enforced from without, but it is a law out of desire and delight of the renewed heart that has truly experienced the living Christ through the inner workings of the Holy Spirit. The believer is ready to obey and puts himself under Christ's Law of Love. The Law of Liberty is aptly named, because the believer who has responded to the workings of the Holy Spirit's conviction, correction, and instruction (like the disciples did) is now free from self-centeredness, and at liberty to simply love.

> *"Now the Lord is the Spirit, and where the Spirit of the Lord is, there is liberty (emancipation from bondage, freedom)."*
> 2 Corinthians 3:17 AMP

A Failure to Love

The apostles addressed serious believers who were being changed by God's love. They had repented of their sins and had come to know the resurrection power of Jesus in their own spirit and soul, through the workings of the indwelling Holy Spirit. They were walking an exchanged life—their life for God's life. They were allowing God to thoroughly deal with them so they could mature in Christlikeness, learning how to love well. However, in our day, the church has received the influence of progressive ideas toward soft-selling sin and relational immorality. The apostles knew how to tell the truth, calling sin what it actually is, instead of dismissing it to protect their flesh life. As a church, we are certainly not walking where they walked in the Kingdom of God's Love. They knew what I want you to learn as well: *Relational immorality is sin, and sin—simply stated—is a self-centered failure to love, and falling short of love is immoral in God's eyes, even wicked and evil.*

Moral evil is any deviation from the rules of conduct prescribed by God, or by legitimate human authority; or any violation of the plain principles of justice and rectitude [right standing with God and others].

> *"Let him turn away from wickedness and shun it, and let him do right. Let him search for peace (harmony; undisturbedness from fears, agitating passions, and moral conflicts) and seek it eagerly. [Do not merely desire peaceful relations with God, with your fellowmen, and with yourself, but pursue, go after them!]"*
>
> 1 Peter 3:11 AMP

This passage tells us that merely being disturbed by fears is wicked, and engaging in stressful moral conflicts (which pertain to relations) is wicked. What Christian is even aware that such things are wicked? We don't as a rule use such harsh language to describe wrong conduct in relationships. Perhaps it's because our consciences have become so de-sensitized by long-term carnal relating patterns, but the definition brings it home.

Where Perverse Thinking Begins

WICKED—The primary sense is to wind and turn, or to depart and fall away. Wicked is any principle or practice deviating from Divine Law. This word is comprehensive, extending to everything contrary to the Moral Law [everything contrary to right-relating practices]. We say things such as a wicked man, a wicked deed, wicked ways, wicked lives, a wicked heart, wicked designs, and wicked works. Wicked is EVIL, sinful, and immoral. The word "evil" suggests bad qualities of a moral kind, which tend to corrupt and pervert.

WICKEDNESS—turning away from right relating with others—leads to corruption and perversion of heart and mind. All thought processes—whether truth or error—begin in the heart with the quality of our morality [heart-level relating]. Our relating habits, such as the way we treat our family members, will either **align us rightly with our Heavenly**

Father or turn us away from Him to devise error, which actually will lead some people to embrace false ideas, false gospels, and other false religious doctrines. It is not the mere influence of an idea or doctrine that leads people to sin, but the sin in people's hearts that leads to the formation of perverse doctrines and substitute emphases. Jesus said, *"But whatever comes out of the mouth comes from the heart, and this is what makes a man unclean and defiles [him]" (Matthew 15:18).*

In a Fog of Error

If you think perversion of mind doesn't apply to you, let me assure you that if you do not relate rightly with your loved ones, your thinking is skewed in many ways, and you are being influenced by the lies of the enemy. Twisted, perverse thinking among Christians is entirely too common. They often possess a melting pot of ideas and beliefs that support and minister to their own brand of pride and fleshly ways. Their beliefs often contradict each other, but they are completely unaware of it. A void of instruction in the Law of Love—where people are helped to recognize and repent of relational sin—*always* results in twisted thinking about truth.

My Story ~ "The Fog Lifts"

In January 1988, I experienced a truly complete baptism of the Holy Spirit. I experienced a washing in the Lord's loving presence. He changed me at the very core of my being. My new daily experience was being loved by the Lord, and I came to see how I wasn't loving the people in my life. My new spiritual baptism was empowering me for the overcoming and obedient life in Christ—learning how to love people. For four years God had been showing me so many of my relational wrongs, and I had been cooperating with His work in my life as fully as I knew how, but little did I know the worst of it was yet to come, but also the best blessings of all.

It was now Spring—a time for new beginnings, and I had had no idea I was placing so many wrong expectations on my dear husband, Jim. I believed I had been right and was making an accurate appraisal of a trying situation and so thought my demands toward him were reasonable…

> *"If you do not relate rightly with your loved ones, your thinking is skewed in many ways, and you are being influenced by the lies of the enemy."*

One day as Jim was leaving for work, I was crying—again. As I cried on his shoulder and clung to him, I begged him to do something about this trying situation that I was convinced at that time he could do something about. I was unable to hear and understand him due to my emotional neediness. Crying to Jim as he was walking out the door to work was becoming a daily event. The Lord, however, was getting my attention, and that day after Jim left, the Holy Spirit corrected me and provided instruction. The next time I was tempted to do such a thing, I was to keep my emotional pleas to myself, and after Jim left I was to go into the bathroom and pour it all out to the Lord.

The next day God's love empowered me to obey, and thus began the pattern of daily pouring out my frustrations, my emotions, and my concerns to God. At first, I didn't understand it, but I was actually going to the cross in heartfelt repentance, becoming emptied of selfish ways and self-centeredness. What surprised me during that initial few months, was that God was actually responding to me. Since I began to thank Him in my distress, He began filling me with Himself. I wasn't even aware of it at the time just how much I was changing; it would be several months before I noticed, but I was maturing from the inside out. My heart and mind were becoming renewed in love, truth was being clarified, and the fog of error completely lifted from my life.

God accomplished a deep cleansing of my soul and I began learning how to love much and love well. I was a new person and I loved the Lord with my whole heart! My emotional makeup not only stabilized but became completely balanced. I continued to grow strong in the Lord from that day forward as I learned how to be deeply grateful, trusting God for everything.

When We Can't See Jesus

When we don't enter into God's ways of working in our lives, we never come to see who He really is—His character and holiness. We simply can't know Him. When we can't see God's true identity, we devise substitute gospels to serve. This is way more common than you might think! Twisted interpretations of Scripture blanket whole segments of the church in a fog of error. You can actually begin to wonder about all the truth you may be misunderstanding when you see that your relational fruit is not what it should be.

Walking in the light of truth is the only way scales will fall from our spiritual eyes. The Scripture shows us how, when we can't see Jesus, we reduce God's image to something our natural mind can comprehend. We look at God through the lens of our flesh, resulting in the lack of desired relational fruit and influence toward faith and moral character we want with our children.

> *"Thus they exchanged Him Who was their Glory for the image of an ox that eats grass [they traded their Honor for the image of a calf]!"*
>
> Psalm 106:20

What happened here?! When the Israelites left Egypt to go into the wilderness to worship God, it was God Himself who called them and brought them out of Egypt. They were supposed to wait for His directive in *how* to do what He was calling them to do. Like children, they were presumptuous and impatient. They decided to worship Him the only way *they* knew how, according to Egyptian patterns. They worshipped according to their own fleshly ideas about God's identity, instead of according to the Spirit's revelation of a loving Heavenly Father and a Holy God. They sinned against God and each other, opening the door to demonic influence in their worship.

This bears understanding because many today fall into a similar trap. God had not yet given them the Law, which was given to expose their personal need, and to raise holy standards of conduct and behavior, demonstrating some important relational principles. They were in bondage to all their own ways, and so, in getting ahead of God, they reduced Him down to something they could understand—the mere image of a calf! What He wanted was a relationship!

The Israelites didn't even know God yet. If they had waited for God to reveal himself, they would have seen their own nakedness and need, come to repentance, and God would have removed the veil of the flesh that created the barrier in their understanding of who He is. *"But whenever a person turns [in repentance] to the Lord, the veil [of the flesh] is taken away"* (2 Corinthians 3:16). If they had simply obeyed Him—repented of their own ways—they would have experienced His forgiveness and His glory—His love.

Can you imagine worshipping a molten image?! Modern Christians would agree this seems stupid and senseless. The real, living God for a calf! We may be more sophisticated today, but some really do much the same thing—worshipping God according to their *own* ideas of the Gospel without actually knowing God. Some streams of the church serve up a false gospel, unknowingly deceiving their followers.

False Gospels and False Ideas

False gospels and false ideas are always void of the needed instruction in Christ's Law of Love, claiming that if you follow or obey another prescribed religious path it proves you are loving God. Believers accept His relational value system in theory but deny it in practicality. In turn, they deny the power of the resurrection to do anything real in their souls, saying that we can never really achieve righteousness but we're just supposed to keep trying. Even in segments of the church where the resurrection is acknowledged and believed, believers are rarely taught how to apply faith toward any practical inner workings of the Holy Spirit and the overcoming life. The Gospel—the Good News—is replaced with various substitute emphases that are attributed to the Holy Spirit, but won't bring true inner change to people's lives, rendering the church powerless. What all this means is that if the true Gospel of reconciliation and the Holy [purely loving] relational value system it stands for is not being preached there is a strong possibility you are in error.

> *"False gospels and false ideas are always void of Christ's Law of Love. They virtually deny the power of the resurrection to do anything real in people's souls."*

You may have experienced God and His presence through one or more spiritual disciplines, such as prayer, Bible study, worship, deeper levels of community life through small groups, serving the less fortunate, receiving prophetic insight from another believer, and so on. Standing alone, any one of these pursuits can seem to have an influence for growth in your life, but it's more likely they may only be providing you with a spiritual reason for not doing the hard work of maturing. Your Christian life can still be characterized as "emotionally unhealthy spirituality" that is not contributing anything good to your salvation.

Emotionally Unhealthy Spirituality

Peter Scazzero, founder and pastor of New Life Church in Queens, New York City and author of *The Emotionally Healthy Church* and *Emotionally Healthy Spirituality*, found:

> *"The spirituality of most current discipleship models often only adds an additional protective layer against people growing up emotionally. Because people are having real, and affirming, spiritual experiences in certain areas of their lives—such as worship, prayer, Bible studies, and fellowship—they mistakenly believe they are doing fine, even if their relational life and interior world is not in order. This apparent "progress" then provides a spiritual reason for not doing the hard work of maturing. They are deceived."*

But Jesus made it clear that the Christian life is made up of much more than a religious value system and spiritual disciplines or isolated experiences with God. It is one of inner growth and change that allows us to positively influence others for God—including and beginning with the work of influencing our own children. True spiritual growth is profoundly practical, bringing about much positive relational change in a person's life. Any discipleship effort should support and promote heart-level growth and change so believers' lives can be transformed.

The seeming void of teaching the true Gospel doesn't mean that leaders assume people already get it, and now they're to move on to more interesting matters. The void of instruction in true gospel principles actually exposes the substitute emphases for building and living the Christian life. Believers are instead taught to add spiritual knowledge and church activity on top of their unaddressed flesh issues, which keeps their moral character in a childish state and their minds unrenewed in a fog of error. A true biblical renewal of the mind is not about gaining head knowledge and information, but it can only begin with heart-level changes that heal relationships, and in turn, impact the process of renewal that transforms life as it ought. Substituting for the real deal is common because many leaders do not know how to provide relational discipleship on a church-wide basis or even an individual one. They have to resort to programs that only teach biblical and spiritual knowledge, which doesn't contribute to heart-level growth and change.

Substitute Emphases for Spiritual Life

Substitute emphases can be as simple as a church with a heavy emphasis on witnessing, or an emphasis on exercising the gifts of the Holy Spirit, or on lots of Bible study and teachings. Even some inner healing ministries can be faulted for telling people what they want to hear, keeping their followers in a perpetual state of circumventing their conscience, instead of leading them to reconcile their relationships at the heart level bringing true healing to their lives. Believers come to think that these activities are what make them mature when in reality they are still children in need of training. *Wrong moral behavior in relationships with people [unholiness and unloving relating] leads to replacing the truth that should be taught, resulting in leaders and lay believers alike believing they are living the Christian life, when in fact they are not.*

The only strong emphasis Christians are supposed to have is Love. Learning how to love much and to love well is our goal and our purpose. Love energizes our duties and good works with the correct spirit, the correct motivations, intentions, and attitudes. This emphasis challenges everything we think we are. When Love's standard is raised in the church, not only is immorality exposed but doctrinal error along with it.

If you've built your religious life around a strong emphasis on one of the following, to the exclusion of the believer's true purpose, you have embraced a false gospel and are in danger of missing out on the power of the true Gospel of Jesus Christ:

- ***accumulating bible knowledge that doesn't contribute to heart-level growth***

> *"You search and investigate and pore over the Scriptures diligently, because you suppose and trust that you have eternal life through them. And these [very Scriptures] testify about Me! And still you are not willing [but refuse] to come to Me, so that you might have life."*
>
> John 5:39-40 AMP

Your form of fellowship with other believers will follow points of argument, and your attempts to influence others will be toward issues of importance to you instead of what is important to Christ—the ministry of reconciliation. This, my friend, feeds your pride and is wicked and immoral. Paul said to know nothing but Jesus Christ crucified.

- *gender-specific doctrines*

> "There is [now no distinction] neither Jew nor Greek, there is neither slave nor free, there is not male and female; for you are all one in Christ Jesus."
>
> Galatians 3:28 AMP

Your perverse understanding of submission will produce a false unity and poor relational fruit in your marriage. It will prevent true spiritual growth because it enables irresponsibility toward personal truth-telling and accountability. This, my friend, is contrary to the Gospel of Liberty Christ won for all.

- *authoritarian leadership structures*

> "You know that those who are recognized as governing and are supposed to rule the Gentiles (the nations) lord it over them [ruling with absolute power, holding them in subjection], and their great men exercise authority and dominion over them. But this is not to be so among you; instead, whoever desires to be great among you must be your servant."
>
> Mark 10:42-43 AMP

> "Not that we have dominion [over you] and lord it over your faith, but [rather that we work with you as] fellow laborers [to promote] your joy, for in [your] faith (in your strong and welcome conviction or belief that Jesus is the Messiah, through Whom we obtain eternal salvation in the kingdom of God) you stand firm."
>
> 2 Corinthians 1:24 AMP

Controlling and being controlled keep people in a perpetual state of emotional and spiritual immaturity and irresponsibility. It produces anger in relationships that leads to resentment and strife. This, my friend, does not allow the Holy Spirit to be in control. Nor does this behavior trust God's work in others.

- *faith applied to everything except to growth and change toward Christlike character formation*

> "For this very reason, adding your diligence [to the divine promises], employ every effort in exercising your faith to develop virtue (excellence, resolution, Christian energy), and in [exercising] virtue [develop] knowledge (intelligence)..."
> 2 Peter 1:5 AMP

Your misapplied faith is turned away from Truth, the person of Jesus Christ, which puts you in danger of being in error. This, my friend, is wicked and immoral.

Calling Evil Evil

Twisted thinking about truth is evil. Furthermore, harshness with children is wicked, evil, and immoral. Unwillingness to mend misunderstandings is both wicked and evil. Unkindness is wicked, and all selfish thought processes and actions are evil and immoral. All unloving actions are wicked and immoral. Failing to bring needed correction to your children because of self-centered fears and emotions or distractions is wicked. Forcing an appearance of unity through controlling behaviors and false submission practices is immoral because it winds and turns you and your loved ones away from truth along a wicked way, violating the conscience of everyone trapped in these patterns. Engaging in chronic self-pity is wicked. Placing unfitting expectations on yourself or others is immoral.

These sorts of moral issues stem from a relative personal morality where we have set our own standards for what is acceptable behavior in an effort to protect our own flesh and keep it alive. The church is unaccustomed to calling what is actually evil, evil. Isaiah warned of woe to those who called evil good.

> *"Woe to those who draw [calamity] with cords of iniquity and falsehood, who bring punishment to themselves with a cart rope of wickedness,...Woe to those who call evil good and good evil, who put darkness for light and light for darkness, who put bitter for sweet and sweet for bitter! Woe to those who are wise in their own eyes and prudent and shrewd in their own sight!"*
> Isaiah 5:18; 20-21 AMP

Going After Peaceful Relations

Woe is a sorrowful experience of grief and calamity brought on by our own wickedness in relation to others. It's common for unteachable people to cause a lot of strife in relationships, harming and even destroying the relationships that mean the most to them. The Scripture doesn't just warn us to turn away from wickedness and shun it, it goes further and exhorts us to intentionally go after peaceful relations with everyone. Not merely desire them, but to go after them. Here it is again:

> *"...Let him search for peace (harmony; undisturbedness from fears, agitating passions, and moral conflicts) and seek it eagerly. [Do not merely desire peaceful relations with God, with your fellowman, and with yourself, but pursue, go after them!]"*
> 1 Peter 3:11 AMP

When people pursue a false sense of peace by trying to "keep the peace" without effectively addressing the relational problems that caused the strife to begin with, they still experience underlying tensions, agitations, and disturbances. In *true* peaceful and loving relationships, these are non-existent! In the rare times when something does begin to come up, it is quickly and truthfully addressed among all parties involved so loving understanding can be restored.

God's Promise

And God gives us a promise that if we turn away from our wicked ways, He will heal the "land" of our lives—everything pertaining to our personal realm of influence.

> *"If My people, who are called by My name, shall humble themselves, pray, seek, crave, and require of necessity My face and turn from their wicked ways, then will I hear from heaven, forgive their sin, and heal their land."*
>
> 2 Chronicles 7:14 AMP

What We Must Do

God is personal and works in a relationship with anyone who will believe Him. To learn how to love much and to love well, we must learn to call relational immorality what it is—sin—naming it, and repenting of our own wickedness, because all sin is simply a failure to love. Sin begins in the attitudes, intentions, and motivations of the heart—why we do and say what we do and say. What a work we need in our hearts! What is your attitude toward your children when you are impatient with them? What is your attitude when you are glad that school will start again soon so you can be free of them? What is your intention when you harshly rebuke your child for interrupting you at the computer? Why are you treating them the way you are?

I have a question for you. Are you even available to Him for this work? In fact, you may be excusing yourself right now, but I hope you are more fully aware that the Lord may have been trying to get your attention to these matters for quite some time. And I hope you are choosing to come to Him so that you might have LIFE.

God's Heart-Level Plan

We must see the need for a deeper examination of the heart, because, unlike in Old Testament times when God dealt with His people by their *outward conduct out of compliance*, His dealings with New Testament believers are based upon *inward heart motivation out of love*. God now only deals with us based on this new plan—His work in us through the Holy Spirit—*"... I'm writing out the plan in them, and carving it on their hearts"* (Hebrews 8:6).

> *"If we are not connecting with Him in this effort, then we are not connecting with Him at all."*

The plan was set in place by Jesus' finished work on the cross, but it is now given to us to cooperate with the transfer of this work into our own hearts. *If we are not connecting with Him in this effort to become loving in our attitudes, intentions, and motivations, then we are not connecting with Him at all, which exposes our self-centeredness and makes our religious activity and our Christian faith suspect.* He only works through His plan—through His indwelling Holy Spirit—convicting our conscience of His will to increase us in His love. Any other work, and by any other name, simply doesn't belong to Him, including the work of diligent Bible study, aggressive witnessing, mysterious spiritual activity, and trying to be good apart from His work in our hearts. Jesus said:

> *"You search and investigate and pore over the Scriptures diligently, because you suppose and trust that you have eternal life through them. And these [very Scriptures] testify about Me!*

And still you are not willing [but refuse] to come to Me, so that you might have life."

John 5:39

The life Jesus refers to is always about His Moral Law of Love—receiving love and walking in love in our relationships, beginning with our spouse and children. So you see, God didn't do away with His plan for righteousness when He shifted focus from the Old Testament Law to the New Law of Love. He merely changed His outworking of it, personalizing it through the work of the indwelling Holy Spirit, correcting and instructing us in the multiple *particulars* of our relating habits with Him and the people in our lives. He has provided grace through Jesus Christ, not as a license to follow any righteousness standard that ministers to our pride and makes us feel good, but as the means to transfer His Moral Law of Love into our hearts where we can become overcomers and intimately experience His love, and thereby learn to love others.

A Merciful Reminder ~ *Heart attitudes, intentions, and motivations toward others tell the truth about the quality of your morality.*

~ Sobering Reality ~
Heart attitudes, intentions, and motivations toward others tell the truth about the quality of your morality.

Testimonies

Tim describes the heart-level sins he discovered while examining his life against the Law of Love, and how those self-seeking motivations manifested in his relationships.

> *I was very insecure and constantly afraid of looking stupid. This insecurity permeated every area of my life all the time—home, work, church, and in every relationship. When I saw someone doing something that I would feel stupid about if I were doing it, I was quick to criticize that person as being stupid. I tore people down to make myself feel better about myself. I did this mostly in my mind, but I spoke my criticism at and about my wife.*
>
> *Also in my mind I used women to bolster my sense of male superiority. I assumed that I knew why people did what they did without trying to understand, and it was usually because they were inferior in some way. I did this most aggressively with my wife. I judged and blamed her as having hurtful motivations toward me. I accused her of lying to me, being uncaring toward my concerns, deliberately making things difficult for me, and not loving me because she did not fulfill what I thought were her duties. What I was really doing is projecting all my own insecurities, false expectations, and judgments onto others. They would never be able to live up to my unloving expectations.*
>
> *My insecurity led me to talk about my job constantly because I believed it proved that I was a smart and good man. My constant insecurity also led me to have an insatiable need to tear someone down. I used my wife and kids for this purpose. They could never live up to my unrealistic image of the good little family that should be waiting for me when I came home*

from work so I showered them with verbal disapproval and criticism in anger, frustration and ridicule.

> "Because I was uptight with my wife and the kids, I didn't want to be affectionate with them. If they tried to be affectionate with me, I would respond by being stiff or finding something I needed to do and letting them know they were in my way." ~ Tim

Because I was uptight with my wife and the kids, I didn't want to be affectionate with them. If they tried to be affectionate with me, I would respond by being stiff or finding something I needed to do and letting them know they were in my way. Frequently I withheld affection from my wife in order to punish her, and if she came close to me or touched me, I would push her away from me with irritation.

My male superiority led me to treat my wife like she lived to meet my every whim and demand, so I aggressively blamed her for everything I perceived as failure in her service to me. I just couldn't let myself be blamed for anything so I had to shift any perceived blame onto someone else. This led me to frequently spew verbal accusations while I was at home, most of them directed at my wife. At times when accusing my wife, if she tried to defend herself or tried to let me know she didn't mean to upset me, I would intensify my attack with harsher, louder, and faster accusations. I refused to believe her or listen to her. Then I would emotionally punish her with silence and coldness for a day or two until I wanted something from her.

At that time, I would decide to accept her apology for upsetting me.

Barbie describes the heart-level sins that she discovered as she examined her life against the Law of Love, and how those self-seeking motivations manifested in her relationships, using other people to build herself up.

As I examined my relational habits in light of the Law of Love, I found that I used certain people in order to get approval for myself by habitually doing those things that put me in a good light to them, even at great inconvenience to my family. I was motivated by the love of knowledge and I paraded my knowledge, making people feel small even though I told myself I was trying to help people. I was motivated by self-protection and I avoided conflict. I operated in a measure of judgment in which I held myself to an unrealistic standard in my mind without grace. I viewed others, especially my children through this judgment-lens as well, expecting them to be what I considered to be righteous without meeting their true needs.

In my relationships with others outside my family, I wove information about my accomplishments, positions and talents into my conversations so that I could build up my image to the people I was talking to. I thought of this activity as letting others get to know me. If I particularly wanted the approval of a specific person, such as people in church leadership, I would be very in tune with how they perceived me and sometimes I would imagine that things they said or did were meant as rejection for me, and feel very hurt about that.

Within my family, I found that I used my children to make an image of myself as a good Christian parent. I was pleased with how they appeared to be responsible and helpful people at church. At home when they did not fit into this image of how they ought to be, I broadcast signs of disapproval to them. Since I was unhappy with them, I didn't feel like being affectionate so I wasn't. I held them to some unrealistic standards without much grace. In protecting myself from conflict, I would apologize for things I didn't do that my husband blamed me for and manipulate circumstances attempting to keep him from getting mad at me. I also would let people in my life continually sin against me. I would not tell them the truth about what they were doing, because I feared they would get upset with me or blame me for hurting their feelings. I liked to think that I could help people with their problems, but I was really using them to parade knowledge and build myself up.

> "I used to think that my efforts toward appeasing or preventing my husband's anger were about being a submitted wife. I believed I was being his helper." ~ Barbie

Barbie describes what she used to think or say about her behaviors that she now calls sin, evil, wicked, and unloving.

I came to see that I was being an enabler for my husband's anger. I was helping to hold him captive in his anger by trying to fix the things that seemed to make him angry and taking on the blame for his anger by apologizing so we could be peaceful again, when I should have been confronting his anger, and allowing the blame to stay with him where it belonged. I used to think that my efforts toward appeasing or preventing my husband's anger were about being a submitted wife. I believed I was being his helper, which fit in with my faulty understanding of what it means to be a godly wife. In reality, I wasn't helping him though. My actions allowed him to continue controlling our home environment with his anger, and allowed him to continue to blame me. I thought taking on blame and being the one to apologize was being a humble peacemaker. I wasn't making real peace though, just a temporary break in the outbursts. Real peace would come when my husband began to repent, and I stopped trying to get my approval from him. I learned that allowing others to blame me for things I didn't do, and being motivated by accusation is self-seeking and unloving.

I thought of my efforts toward getting the approval of church leaders as serving God by serving the church. I thought of my love of knowledge as wisdom from God and necessary to help people become more like me in their lifestyle choices, because I thought of myself as a model Christian. I subconsciously believed that parading my accomplishments and talents would make people like me more. If they liked me more, they would come to church with me so I thought of the process as serving God by creating interest in becoming more like people who go to church. I learned that expecting or trying to get the attention and approval from others is unloving.

I thought that my disapproval of my children would motivate them to do better at what I wanted them to do. I thought making them feel ashamed would change their behavior. I thought that by avoiding confrontation with people who were sinning against me, I was extending God's grace, and "covering over a multitude of sin" but really I was just nursing my own fear of making people upset with me. I was more concerned about my feelings of being rejected than I was about the controlling people and the truth they needed to become free from their sin. I learned that fear of confronting and correcting someone is self-seeking and unloving.

Tim *and* ***Barbie*** describe how they worshipped God in their flesh before they started to know Him.

> ***Tim*** *Outwardly I did all the things I thought a good Christian ought to do. I spent time reading my Bible and praying in personal devotional times. I went to church three times a week and was always involved in church activities. I went to men's Bible studies and I tithed regularly. I rarely, if ever, worshipped on my own. Worship was out of duty and not relationship. These things didn't produce a real and vital personal relationship with the Lord, so I still wanted to feel close to God. At times I sought after some sort of spiritual high. I wanted to have spiritual experiences that would make me feel emotionally good about myself by escaping my true spiritual condition, which was based on duty. At times through the years I felt a brief closeness to God, but those times were few and far between.*
>
> ***Barbie*** *I sang and made music in Christian settings a great deal. I felt comfortable singing things about God's greatness and His sovereignty. I was less comfortable with songs of personal love. I did not really worship the Lord by myself very often. It felt empty to me, and I focused on my own voice or instrument playing instead of on the Lord. I thought the Lord's focus was on inviting people to church, and getting people to like church so they wouldn't leave. I served God in that fashion, trying to get people to like me so they would go to church with me, and working hard to make church a likeable place. I studied the Bible in order to get more knowledge and satisfy my idea of a requirement for a devotional time.*

8 Challenging Ideas and Corresponding Sobering Realities

Challenging Idea #1 ~ *Most Christian parents don't know what moral and spiritual training consists of and are leaving it to chance.*

Sobering Reality #1 ~ *You are being told on by your own relational fruit, but the hope is that God wants to empower you to change your fruit.*

Challenging Idea #2 ~ *Morality is the heart-level quality of how people relate with each other, defining character as the sum of our relational habits.*

Sobering Reality #2 ~ *The state of your relationships defines your character and reflects your true spiritual condition. You are your children's character education.*

Challenging Idea #3 ~ *It's impossible to transfer moral values in broad generalities that are unrelational. They are successfully instilled only by addressing the particulars of your family's heart-level relating habits and patterns.*

Sobering Reality #3 ~ *A biblical morality is clearly defined in all of its relational particulars.*

Challenging Idea #4 ~ *True spiritual growth occurs when we bring our particular morality in line with Christ's Law of Love, making our instruction in moral rectitude completely relational.*

Sobering Reality #4 ~ *Love's evidence [God's standard for moral fruit] is seen in the sacrificial quality of the heart-level attitudes, intentions, and motivations of your relating practices.*

Challenging Idea #5 ~ *Relational immorality is sin, and sin—simply stated—is a self-centered failure to love, and falling short of love is immoral in God's eyes, even wicked and evil.*

Sobering Reality #5 ~ *Heart attitudes, intentions, and motivations toward others tell the truth about the quality of your morality.*

Chapter 6

A Return to Conscience

> *~ A Challenging Idea and Sobering Reality #6 ~*
> *"God gives us the Law of Love, a powerful tool to accomplish two practical purposes—to know ourselves and to know Him."*
> *~ Conscience is the most sacred of all your personal property.*

We've seen that the standard for our morality is God's Law of Love, that moral rectitude is about the *quality* of the way we relate with the people in our lives, as it issues from the attitudes, intentions, and motivations of our hearts. We've taken a look at how morality is transferred to children. Let's turn now to examine how God begins a heart-level work in us so we can make the necessary changes in what we are passing to our children. We need to see the *quality* of morality we are actually modeling for them. We need to examine ourselves according to our particular morality and come into alignment with God's Moral Law of Love. When we are properly reconciled, we'll be able to transfer truth to our children.

Forming Moral Rectitude Begins with Reconciliation

The big picture of what God is doing is about reconciliation—restoring all things to Himself. Gospel truths are about reconciliation with God and with others, bringing life into harmony. The Scriptures are clear that making things right between people is the ministry entrusted to us. I include both The Amplified and The Message versions here to provide more clarity.

> *"But all things are from God, Who through Jesus Christ reconciled us to Himself [received us into favor, brought us into harmony with Himself] and gave to us the ministry of reconciliation [that by word and deed we might aim to bring others into harmony with Him]. It was God [personally present] in Christ, reconciling and restoring the world to favor with Himself, not counting up and holding against [men] their trespasses [but canceling them], and committing to us the message of reconciliation (of the restoration to favor)."*
>
> 2 Corinthians 5:18-19 AMP

> *"Now we look inside, and what we see is that anyone united with the Messiah gets a fresh start, is created new. The old life is gone; a new life burgeons! Look at it! All this comes from the God who settled the relationship between us and Him, and then called us to settle our relationships with each other. God put the world square with Himself through the Messiah, giving the world a fresh start by offering forgiveness of sins. God has given us the task of telling everyone what He is doing. We're Christ's representatives. God uses us to persuade men and women to drop their differences and enter into God's work of making things right between them. We're speaking for Christ himself*

now: Become friends with God; He's already a friend with you."

The Message

Since God created reality and how life is supposed to work, He is in the business of reconciling us to His ways of developing the central area of our lives—relationships. He sets the guidelines for how relationships work and wants to bring us back to the way moral rectitude is formed and how inner growth works so we can make our relationships whole. Coming into alignment with His ways of relating will reconcile us to Him in wholeness and in harmony.

Reconciliation Begins with Self-Examination

God provides a powerful beginning for forming moral rectitude [for our hearts becoming Christlike (sanctified)] and subsequent equipping as parents. He begins by drawing us into engaging with Him in a process of self-examination. We can see that our self-examination is not in the light of just any old standard of our own making, based upon what feels good to us, but in the light of His character, goodness, and holiness. Our standard should be based not on a moral standard that is *general*, but is actually quite *particular* in nature because God's character is made up of many particulars and He created us to know Him.

We have to have intimate knowledge of God's character and understand His ways of relating if His love is to impact the quality of how we relate with others [the quality of our morality]. However, I will say it again, coming to know God intimately begins with the need for intimate knowledge of our own ways (our relating habits) in order to receive needed course corrections from God so the reconciliation process can begin as we come into proper alignment with Him.

Self-Examination Acquaints Us with Our Own Sin, Using a Powerful Tool God Gives

We can't be rightly aligned with Him without first becoming acquainted with our own sin nature and dispositions toward the flesh [ways and behavior practices that oppose God and produce bad relational fruit]. We have to learn how to love as He loves, and our baggage is in the way of doing so. I am not suggesting uncovering everything that ever happened to a person that may have caused all their hurts and wounds so they can "nurse it and rehearse it" to feel justified in their own sin. This form of self-examination—or historical review—can circumvent the conscience and keep the person stuck in self-centeredness.

I am suggesting learning to recognize how the neglect of particular moral training and the wounding we received throughout childhood may have actually led us into sin or at least left us ignorant about how to overcome, which in turn caused us to hurt others. Our own immorality is what needs to be addressed, and this can only be accomplished through the examination of conscience. And so, I want you to understand this message's main idea: *God gives us the Law of Love, a powerful tool to accomplish two practical purposes—to know ourselves and to know Him.*

Building our relationship with God in truth about ourselves allows us to begin to glimpse His holiness, which is simply experiencing His love. He wants us to know Him, but we must come to see our own unholiness—unloving ways—and repent. Scripture tells us that the Law is given for this very purpose, to help us to know ourselves.

> *"For [the real function of] the Law is to make men recognize and be conscious of sin [not mere perception, but an acquaintance with sin which works toward repentance, faith, and holy character]."*
>
> Romans 3:20 AMP

Acquaintance is more than merely knowing about someone or something. It is more than slight or superficial knowledge. It is *familiar* and *intimate* knowledge. Paul tells us that we are to become *intimately* knowledgeable about our own sin so we can repent. In giving the Law of Love, God wants to accomplish two purposes. The Law not only provides a tool to help us come to know ourselves, but the same tool also helps us to know Him. In reality—the way it actually works—we cannot know God or take on His moral character, grow up spiritually, emotionally, and relationally until we begin to walk in truth about ourselves, abandoning our own ways.

> *"No one who [habitually] sins has either seen or known Him [recognized, perceived, or understood Him, or has had an experiential acquaintance with Him]."*
>
> 1 John 3:6 AMP

Truth-telling aligns us properly so we can get to know God. Repentance alone is what brings us into moral rectitude and proper alignment with God so we can know Him. This is why God always begins our relationship with Him by convicting us of sin so we can begin the process of self-examination and repentance.

A Personal Example ~ The Wrong Approach to Self-Examination

Some preachers have said that self-examination is "morbid." This may be in response to the perverse processes of self-examination that have been common in our culture and among secular help groups. I had a personal experience with this when I inherited dozens of journals that had belonged to my adopted daughter's deceased mother. She spent much of her short life in rehabilitation programs. Her journals were definitely morbid and self-destructive, yet she was encouraged by the "experts" to journal in such a way.

People who have been deeply wounded and disturbed or destroyed their life through drugs are sometimes led to "dump" their feelings about what others did to them, but instead of providing the healing forgiveness they really need, it actually leads them to perpetually glorify their negative experiences, making them into a sort of god. They rehearse and live in their stuff, spinning their wheels going nowhere.

My adopted daughter, who had also been involved in help groups, was already engaged in similar activities when she came to live with us at barely fifteen years of age. I gently removed her journals and taught her how to forgive and put her past behind her so she could embrace her present need for healing. I focused on addressing her own relational [moral] issues so she could experience God's grace and merciful forgiveness, and only occasionally made connections for her regarding how she had been treated so she could understand why her soul was dysfunctional. However, the focus was always on her responsibility to learn how to respond correctly.

A time came when she was healed enough in love to revisit parts of her past so she could increase in understanding, and experience further healing of memories. This was a process led by the work of the Holy Spirit in her life, but after she chose to develop her relationship with God, and in the context of open and truthful relationships with family members, especially with me, her mom. It was a healthy process, bringing her into wise maturity, and forming in her a sound mind that thinks right about life.

> *"It's not our hurts and wounds we measure or examine, but how we've hurt and wounded others."*

What Self-Examination Looks At or Measures

Scripture provides the measuring rod for a correct examination of conscience. It's not our hurts and wounds we measure or examine (how others have hurt us and why we feel hurt by them), but how we've hurt and wounded others. For true believers in Jesus Christ, the measuring rod by which we examine our own lives and actions is the Law of Love that Jesus gave us in the Two Commandments, which when obeyed fulfills the Old Covenant requirements for right living. Our inner healing comes only from being reconciled to His ways of love.

> *"You shall love the Lord your God with all your heart and with all your soul and with all your mind (intellect). This is the great (most important principle) and first commandment. And a second is like it: You shall love your neighbor as [you do] yourself. These two commandments sum up and upon them depend the Law and the Prophets."*
> Matthew 22:37-40 AMP

Jesus fulfilled all the requirements for righteousness and moral rectitude, by obeying and loving perfectly. His sacrifice made available to us, through the gift of the Holy Spirit, the power to overcome sin [self-centeredness] so we can learn to love much and love well, and thereby cooperate with God's work of sanctification [inner growth in holiness and love] toward moral rectitude in our lives, becoming genuinely reconciled.

God's standards cause us to examine two things in our personal lives: the *moral character* [the sum of our relational habits] and the *faith* of our family, both of which require a relational effort to develop.

If you want intellectual children, you measure their command of complex information and ideas. If you want athletes, you measure how committed they are to the physical disciplines required to become great. If you want social children, you measure their likability with their peers. Social skills and popularity are never equated with relational skills, however. In fact, God's Word doesn't even address them. And so, if you want children who love each other, possess Christlike moral character and deep unfeigned faith, you measure the family's internal relational dynamics. We must recognize our current behavior that produced the poor relational fruit we currently live with, and learn to tell the truth about it so God can begin to do a deep cleansing of our hearts and healing of our souls.

No Other Law or Standard

There is no other law or standard by which God wants us to measure ourselves. You may think this is easy enough, since what parent doesn't already love their children? But remember, mere outward compliance with the Law was never what God was after. The Law of Love has to reach the arena of the heart—the place where the quality of our morality is formed. The heart is the seat of intimate relationship with God and with people. It's our inner driving force, and as such the heart attitudes, intentions, and motivations that direct our familial relational patterns are the place to start with our self-examination of conscience. We need to begin to listen to our conscience about the way we love or fail to love. When self-examination is carried on properly, many parents would come to learn just how shockingly self-centered they've been in relationship with their precious children.

Self-Examine to Measure Faith that Shows Proper Fruit

Paul exhorted the Corinthians to measure their progress in the faith.

> *"Examine and test and evaluate your own selves to see whether you are holding to your faith and showing the proper fruits of it."*
>
> 2 Corinthians 13:5

Here, faith is linked with the fruits of the Spirit [Christlike moral character]. We don't examine ourselves according to how much we've been hurt or in light of what others are doing or in light of what makes us feel good, but in light of what God's Word says about how He wants us to relate because God's work in us is all about growing good spiritual fruit, which is always about our relational patterns of behavior. And we examine ourselves to see if we are increasing in our experience of applying truth to our relationships, bringing about deep heart-level change that conforms us to Christlikeness [holy, completely loving, moral character].

God Invites Us into a Two-Part Process ~ to Know Ourselves and to Know His Love

This brings us to the scriptural process in which God asks us to cooperate with Him so He can bring us into His reality to accomplish two good works. God established the order for coming to know Him. *Repentance* first, then *forgiveness*, and next *reconciliation*. He already made the way possible through Christ. It is up to us to align ourselves correctly with His established order—His way of wanting to work in our lives. Reconciliation will always lead to healing.

1.) To become thoroughly acquainted with Christ's Law of Love [familiar and intimate knowledge of His standards].

2.) To examine our own relational fruit in the light of His Law of Love and tell the truth so we can form new relating patterns of behavior in all the particulars.

Correct Self-Examination Allows God to Work in Us Toward Reconciliation

Obeying the Law of Love is virtually impossible without the work of the Holy Spirit to change our hearts at the deepest level where self-centeredness and immorality rule our being. This human impossibility points to how God wants to work in our lives—at the heart level through relationship, because only He can accomplish what is spiritually impossible. It's impossible because God measures love by its sacrificial qualities in the attitudes, intentions, and motivations of the heart. Bringing our internal motivations in line with Christ's ways of sacrificial relating most certainly means we need His grace for the overcoming life.

To overcome, we must learn to differentiate between sin and the flesh, because one is known by the Law and the other by the Spirit. It is by the Spirit that God gives us revelation of the condition of our own hearts, for our carnal ways—the flesh—can only be seen when God shines the light of His Spirit into our souls.

For example, if we lash out in harshness at our children, we may be convicted about it. This conviction is the Holy Spirit's work in us, exposing the sin. If we enter into self-examination, the Holy Spirit will further convict us of our motivation for the sin so we can be free as we obey in stopping the sin, and repenting of the self-seeking motivation. This is the continuing work of the Holy Spirit that transforms our hearts into Christlikeness.

> *"We really need very little cognitive understanding to do the right thing, because the place of God's influence in us begins with our conscience."*

God works in our life through the inner workings of the Holy Spirit's influence on our conscience (Philippians 2:12-13). The power of God is for such as this: changing our moral character, by addressing our relating patterns so He can touch our hearts with His Love. This is God's wonderful grace. No, we can't understand it, not even after we experience it! It's God's power for salvation—what the Kingdom of Heaven on earth is about— *"moral power and excellence of soul."*

Grace becomes even more daunting when we realize that everything we are is motivated by self-centeredness, for we are utterly corrupt and there is no good thing in us (Romans 7:18). Think about this: The deep tendency toward carnal self-seeking behavior in our hearts that is outworked in our actions is a condition of the heart (the sin nature), and not a sin (action) that needs to be repented of. Remember, that we *do* sin, but our condition suggests that we *are* sin.

We ask how it's possible to repent of everything we are, and this is why we need God to address it with the power of His Spirit because we are utterly incapable of repenting of what we are. God provided a way to free us from self and selfish ways through the cross, to which we have access through Jesus Christ.

We can choose to put to death the deeds of the flesh, practicing dying to self and selfish ways. As we cooperate with this work, we will become less and less tolerant of carnal ways and behavior practices, and increase in desire for holiness as we draw closer to God. When we want holiness [completely loving motivation] badly enough; when we want to identify with Christ badly enough; then, and only then, will we be cleansed in the deep ground of our hearts to live holy as Jesus is holy [purely loving]. And so, even though sin originates in the heart, which seems it could never be eradicated—at least by no effort of our own—it can also die in the heart by the power of God's grace.

God's Heart-Work Is Often Uncomfortable

So while it is supposed to get easier in grace, meaning we don't have to do it all ourselves, we have to let go of control over our lives and allow God to work. This isn't easy, because it presses us outside the comfort of our own ways and any desire to protect our pride and self-image, creating lots of emotional tension. For instance, if you've been an emotionless person lacking in the desire to be physically affectionate, God's way of love will be to come out of your comfortable ways to pour affection and express delight on your family. You'll need to become someone new, which is uncomfortable and may make you feel strange and insecure.

> *"The work of the Gospel in our lives was never meant to make us comfortable, but it was meant to make us free."*

Or if you've been afraid of confrontation and you let people control you, you'll need to become a new person that boldly speaks the truth, and brings loving consequences to those who need them regardless of how they treat you in return. This will be uncomfortable for your habitual ways, but you will only take such actions in love after you've allowed God to deal with your own heart first. God's love is the only way our hearts will ever experience a change powerful enough where His standard for righteousness actually becomes a reality in our lives. It is this work alone—His Love—that can deal a death blow to self-centeredness.

The work of the Gospel in our lives was never meant to make us comfortable, but it was meant to make us free. That's why it's wonderfully good news! It's worth the squirming discomfort that truth brings. Freedom is worth the emotional roller-coaster ride that takes us to the cross where our emotional nature becomes stabilized by the touch of God's love on our hearts, making us real people and authentic Christians. How many believers actually allow God this level of involvement in their lives?

We humans have a tendency to want to maintain control. We'll clean up our outward act to the extent we have the ability in our own power to do so, and until we are satisfied with ourselves without having to become too uncomfortable with self-exposure, true guilt, and humility. A clearly spelled-out set of do's and don'ts shows us the sins we commit. We can repent even while maintaining a prideful posture, basically maintaining control while expecting our spouse to "dance around" our issues.

If we explode with anger, we can repent of the outburst, knowing it was wrong, while inwardly telling ourselves, "If YOU hadn't done THAT, I wouldn't have gotten angry!" We comply with the law while the flesh—the self-life—still rules in a heart that is left untouched by God's grace—keeping ourselves outside of God's plan for how He has chosen to work in our lives. The fruit of not entering into His work will be evident in our familial relationships, and we will never come to see who God really is or experience His love.

Repenting and Obeying Form Moral Rectitude ~ Knowing Our Own Sinfulness and His Holiness

"Applying" the Law of Love to the *particulars* of our relationships is supposed to be a vital, interactive process with God that simultaneously accomplishes both works in us, bringing us to know our own sinfulness *and* to know His character, nature, and holiness [purely loving motivation].

His character is outworked in our relationships by faith through a very simple process of repentance from "dead works." Dead works are any false religious standards of righteousness or self-generated relational habits—substitute actions, behaviors, and activities—that take the place of living God's Love through us, according to His particular moral standards. The Lord will supernaturally purify our conscience from these dead works as we repent.

> *"How much more surely shall the blood of Christ, Who by virtue of [His] eternal Spirit [His own preexistent divine personality] has offered Himself as an unblemished sacrifice to God, purify our consciences from dead works and lifeless observances to serve the [ever] living God?"*
>
> Hebrews 9:14 AMP

Repentance from dead works, while simultaneously taking actions according to God's directive, is the most efficient and powerful way change can come to our family relationships. It is also the only way to come to know who God really is and to experience His grace, mercy, and love. Repentance from dead works is how God purifies our conscience, forms new identity within us, and brings us into security as His child. It is also how He wants to *empower the transfer of moral values and faith.*

Through the transference of His moral character into our hearts, we can in turn enable the transfer of His moral character into the hearts of our children. It all begins with self-examination of conscience that works toward repentance. The Scriptures further admonish us to engage in this process.

Self-Examination and Reconciliation Leading to Experiencing God's Acceptance

One of the Beatitudes also points to this order. Jesus said that the pure in heart shall see God (Matthew 5:8). Angry, unloving people are not acquainted with God, and need to allow Him to purify their hearts and actions so they can come to know His character and holiness. People consumed only with their own interests do not know God. Allowing God to be our Father—as He corrects our heart and instructs us—is actually what begins this purifying, growth process, and brings our spiritual adoption into our reality, resulting in actually feeling secure and *experiencing* our true identity as we come to see God.

Testing Ourselves or Testing God?

Some people who hold out on God, refusing to align themselves with His established order for working in their lives, are actually testing God (instead of themselves), waiting for Him to do something before they'll trust Him with their hearts.

> *"To test and prove yourselves [not Christ]. Do you not yourselves realize and know [thoroughly by an ever-increasing experience] that Jesus Christ is in you—unless you are [counterfeits] disapproved on trial and rejected?"*
>
> 2 Corinthians 13:5

Paul says these are counterfeit Christians. God already proved His love and trustworthiness through the ultimate sacrifice of His Son. He now waits for us to get on board with how He has chosen to work in our lives.

For example, if other people can't trust us, we will not be able to trust them or trust God. When we become trustworthy, learning to tell the truth and treating others based on the truth, we begin to experience God's trustworthiness—His holiness and love—and we feel able to trust Him.

Some people who are cut off from experiencing God's grace are waiting for a miracle from Him that will suddenly cause them to trust Him so they can allow Him access to their heart and life. The miracle God wants to give them is one they are in control of receiving right now. It begins with repentance from their own untrustworthy ways so they can receive God's forgiveness and become reconciled to Him. God's grace is there for this process.

My Story ~ "Shocked into Silence"

After fifteen years of suppressing my conscience and giving my life over to whatever made me feel good, I was shocked when my conscience first came alive. It was like God flipped on a light switch inside my soul. I was pretty dis-equilibrated—emotionally undone. I learned how much pride I'd been in, and how I had hurt other people.

Once I recovered from the initial shock of my true condition, the first thing I remember doing in my heart-level cooperation with God was to quiet my soul and practice submitting to His correction and instruction. I distinctly heard the Lord tell me to silence my justifications and excuses and even my opinions for a season so He could correct my faulty thinking. I was to learn how to doubt myself and my own ways—not relying on my own understanding anymore—and learn how to trust Him and His ways through His personal correction and instruction to my conscience.

There were so many changes I began to make in how I related with my own husband and children, but this one positive action served to position me to be available to hear Him so I could become truly obedient.

> *"The first thing I remember doing in my heart-level cooperation with God was to quiet my soul and practice submitting to His correction and instruction."*

Identifying Relational Patterns that Need Redemption

In looking to God's standard of love (and all the particular relational dynamic that entails), we need to develop enough acquaintance with sin —familiarity and intimate knowledge of our own particular relational patterns—so we can work toward repentance, and build our faith—working through love—toward the developing of holy [purely loving] character [the sum of our relational habits] (Galatians 5:6).

Through a process of self-examination and contemplation, and appropriate relational responses to what God shows you, you learn how to identify relational patterns that still need to be redeemed. You also come to recognize that how you relate with others is a direct reflection of how you've been relating with God, actually defining the quality of your morality [your character].

Christians read many books about spiritual growth and how to experience a real connection with God, but many still never do. Most don't even know that the first place of the Holy Spirit's influence is on the conscience. This is so sad since God made it so very simple. Our entire spiritual life is worked out in our human relationships. This is why God's place of influence in our lives is our morality—human relational patterns of behavior—to bring us closer to Him. I want to demonstrate through another testimony that we really need very little cognitive understanding to do the right thing, because the place of God's influence in us begins within our own conscience.

"Jumpstarting a Conscience"
~ A Personal Story of Ministry

In February of 2006, I found myself offering to pray for an elderly woman in an advanced stage of Alzheimer's disease who was being cared for by her daughter's family.

Noticing the sour and nasty presence this woman contributed to the home atmosphere, and fear of and indifference the family had toward "Gramma," I told my new friend, Barbie, that her mom's soul condition was not a result of the disease itself, but that she couldn't minister to her own spirit, and probably never had such ministry in all the previous decade of being withdrawn, due to cognitive loss.

Once I learned more about the woman's history, her life-long ministry and respected leadership lasting over 40 years in the same church, and her parenting and relational practices, I realized that this dear woman had probably never been properly reconciled to God and to others. The Lord had my heart's attention toward Ellen. Because of my long-term experience with ministering in the arena of the heart and not being afraid of heart-level work, I understood that even though this woman's mind was gone, her real person was still there in her spirit. I knew that her spirit had been asleep and simply needed to be awakened so she could experience conviction of conscience and be led to repent and become reconciled to God and to her family. Barbie seemed dubious but would receive any effort I could give.

And so, after talking to Ellen for a while, her head hanging down on her chest, I laid my hand on her chest, and with a faith that only comes through love, I asked the Lord through the power of the Holy Spirit to awaken her spirit and to jumpstart her conscience to receive the ministry of the Lord. She looked up at me, made eye contact, and listened to what I was saying to her. The Lord now had her attention.

> *"This was the beginning of a miracle that turned into many such miracles of whole periods of time, lasting from one to two hours where Ellen was completely lucid..."*

This was the beginning of a miracle that turned into many such miracles of whole periods of time, lasting for more than an hour where Ellen was completely lucid, holding coherent conversations with me, with her daughter, her other visiting daughters, and with her grandchildren.

Eventually, Barbie received the ministry of prayer for her own mother, and over the next several weeks, Ellen confessed to and asked forgiveness for many *particular* relational behaviors and offenses and noticeably changing from the inside so dramatically that it set off a powerful chain of events in this sweet family toward their own spiritual growth and change.

Her testimony is powerful for several reasons, but consider that her short-term memory lasted for only about ten to twenty seconds. She came to know who was caring for her and their names, her entire soul environment changed, making her a happy person, and full of encouragement toward others. She continued to participate in family life up until she went to heaven nearly four years later. To God be the glory for the great works He continues to do!

Your Spiritual Jumpstart

You don't have to understand everything that is wrong in your life in order to "see" what is wrong and to begin a process of repentance that aligns you correctly with the Father. I urge you to receive a spiritual jumpstart to your own conscience. Simply begin with what He shows your own heart.

The church is in desperate need of a return to conscience and moral rectitude. We need a return to Christ's standards of the Law of Love. To do so, we need a return to conscience as well. We need our conscience to come alive! In The Conscience and Post-Modernism, Fritz Ridenour tells us,

> *"What Christians must do above all else is make a new commitment to biblical truth and morality. There is absolute truth in the Word of God. There is absolute [particular] morality in the teaching of Scripture. And there is the ultimate absolute behind it all—Jesus Christ, who is 'the Way, the Truth, and the Life.'"*

A Merciful Reminder ~ *Conscience is the most sacred of all your personal property.*

Testimonies

Tim describes what he saw when he first began to examine his relational habits with his family in the light of God's standard of Love, and what his behavioral habits revealed about his relationship with God.

> *I came to understand that my self-centered and unloving behavior was actually hurtful to my family. I realized that I was more concerned about how I looked than about how I was treating my wife and children. I heard Marilyn teaching that my relationship with my family was a reflection of my relationship with God. My wife helped me to understand that my outward appearance of righteousness and the trappings of church were more important than real relationship. I thought that as long as I was outwardly doing the right things, I was doing my part, and deep in my heart I didn't believe that God was doing His part. I wanted experience of what my church called the spiritual gifts, and victory over some deep sin in my life, but neither of these was happening. I blamed God and I didn't really trust Him.*

> "I came to understand that my self-centered and unloving behavior was actually hurtful to my family." ~ Tim

Barbie describes what she saw when she first began to examine her relational habits with her family in the light of God's standard of Love, and what her behavioral habits revealed about her relationship with God.

When I first began to examine my family relationships, being careful to listen to my conscience, I saw that I was resistant to meet my mom's true needs. My mom was living with us, and she had advanced Alzheimer's disease. Marilyn was telling me that she needed someone to help her pray, help her read her Bible, look in her eyes, and give her affection much like a child needs, because she couldn't do these things for herself. As Marilyn told me these things, I saw that I didn't really want to do that for her.

Our relationship had never been whole because of the neglect I experienced from her in my childhood. I had resistance in my heart toward her, even though I believed that I had forgiven her intellectually.

As I began to listen to my conscience and discipline myself to meet my mom's true needs despite my own feelings, I began to see how my children held so much fear and unforgiveness in their hearts toward their Grandma as well. I was not watching over their hearts as they had been relating to her. I came to understand that God wanted me to meet my mom's needs for love out of my heart, sacrificing my feelings for the sake of meeting her need. I began to see that my ways were not His ways.

Barbie describes times of receiving instruction from the Lord that brought transformation to her relationships.

The Lord spoke to me about how I was relating with my husband. He convicted my conscience that it was wrong for me to spend thought, time and effort on how to keep him from getting angry. At first, this produced in me a sort of paralyzation the next few times my husband was angry. I knew I was not to rush around trying to fix it, but I didn't know what I was supposed to do instead. I actually stood in the middle of the kitchen doing nothing while he roughly fussed and fumed about. Soon I was able to tell him I wouldn't participate in the conversation he wanted to have when he was angry and accusatory, and I walked away.

The Lord spoke to me again very specifically that I could never, and had never, caused my husband to get angry. His anger was something he was choosing to do in his sin and unloving relational habits. Once I understood this, I had a whole new perspective on the way I had been relating to him, and I was able to see how my previous mode was self-seeking and that I contributed to and encouraged his sin. The Lord began to give me a great deal of revelation that eventually helped my husband to become free of his anger altogether.

The Lord spoke to me about telling my mom that I loved her. I found that hard to say out loud to her. I obeyed and brought myself to say it anyway. It eventually became easy to say.

> "I thought that He wanted me to get people to like me so they would come to church with me, but what He is really interested in is reconciliation between people and between people and Himself." ~ Barbie

The Lord spoke to me about how I had been relating with Him. He brought me to understand that I had not been interested in what He was interested in. I thought that He wanted me to get people to like me so they would come to church with me, but what He is really interested in is reconciliation between people and between people and Himself. I was not seeking His Kingdom; I was seeking what I thought He wanted, but I didn't know the real Him. I had an imagination of Him that I was serving faithfully that wasn't really Him. He helped me to understand how I had developed my imagination of Him through self-seeking processes. I repented and began to learn to see people's need for reconciliation, and how through cooperation with Him I could help them see it for themselves and run toward the Lord.

The Lord spoke to me about how I was judging myself. I had a standard for myself that wasn't from Him. When I felt like I had failed, I kicked myself and blamed myself. I came to understand that He only saw that I needed to learn more wisdom, and He had grace for my process. He wasn't blaming me or kicking me. He showed me that I was sitting in a seat of judgment over myself, assuming His position in my life, effectively deifying myself. I repented and was set free from the self-condemnation I had struggled with for so many years.

Barbie describes some of the relational changes in her family since she began to learn to love well.

Since I've learned about what real love looks like, there have been many changes in my family.

The most extensive change has been in my relationship with my husband. I stopped trying to protect myself from my husband's anger. I stopped rushing around trying to fix things when he was angry, and instead told him he was wrong to be angry. I stopped receiving blame from him and instead I told him he was wrong to blame me. I repented to him for enabling him to treat us badly and for loving myself while leaving him trapped in his sin. I prayed for him to become free, and the Lord gave me a great deal of revelation for him, helping him to understand his sinful patterns. The huge change in his heart and the resulting change in his behavior brought radical change in our entire family dynamic.

I came to understand that my children needed me to pour affection, understanding, and encouragement on them, as well as very basic regular instruction in order for them to be able to obey and to learn to love their siblings and the Lord from their hearts. My oldest son's heart, in particular, was very distant from me by the time he was 13. As I began to lavish affection and approval on him, encouraging him in the small disciplines of his life, he came to a point of confessing his hidden sin to me. He then made an abrupt shift in his heart toward me and toward the Lord in obeying his conscience. He earnestly pursued loving his siblings in very practical ways and thirsting for my instruction and counsel in all areas of his life.

> "I came to understand that my children needed me to pour affection, understanding, and encouragement on them." ~ Barbie

Through this change in my son, I became more aware of the distance of heart in my oldest daughter who was then 14. Her heart was easily drawn toward me and toward the Lord as I poured on the affection and approval that she needed.

I had not yet lost the hearts of my younger children, but now I know that I never will. Previously, my children merely got along without much unkindness or outburst. Now they thoroughly enjoy each other's company, being eagerly interested in each other and their interests, and willingly and generously helping and supporting one another in all their endeavors.

8 Challenging Ideas and Corresponding Sobering Realities

Challenging Idea #1 ~ *Most Christian parents don't know what moral and spiritual training consists of and are leaving it to chance.*

Sobering Reality #1 ~ *You are being told on by your own relational fruit, but the hope is that God wants to empower you to change your fruit.*

Challenging Idea #2 ~ *Morality is the heart-level quality of how people relate with each other, defining character as the sum of our relational habits.*

Sobering Reality #2 ~ *The state of your relationships defines your character and reflects your true spiritual condition. You are your children's character education.*

Challenging Idea #3 ~ *It's impossible to transfer moral values in broad generalities that are unrelational. They are successfully instilled only by addressing the particulars of your family's heart-level relating habits and patterns.*

Sobering Reality #3 ~ *A biblical morality is clearly defined in all of its relational particulars.*

Challenging Idea #4 *~ True spiritual growth occurs when we bring our particular morality in line with Christ's Law of Love, making our instruction in moral rectitude completely relational.*

Sobering Reality #4 *~ Love's evidence [God's standard for moral fruit] is seen in the sacrificial quality of the heart-level attitudes, intentions, and motivations of your relating practices.*

Challenging Idea #5 *~ Relational immorality is sin, and sin—simply stated—is a self-centered failure to love, and falling short of love is immoral in God's eyes, even wicked and evil.*

Sobering Reality #5 *~ Heart attitudes, intentions, and motivations toward others tell the truth about the quality of your morality.*

Challenging Idea #6 *~ God gives us the Law of Love, a powerful tool to accomplish two practical purposes—to know ourselves and to know Him.*

Sobering Reality #6 *~ Conscience is the most sacred of all your personal property.*

Chapter 7

God's Top-Down, Inside-Out Approach to Parenting

~ Challenging Idea and Sobering Reality # 7 ~
"God wants to influence you toward heart-level change before you try to change your children—a top-down, inside-out approach that provides understanding and wisdom for parenting."
~ As God parents you, so parent your children.

Personal Story — "An Ill Fit"

Most parents want to change their children. I know I did! I've always loved to dance, and so when my first daughter was only four years old (before I had a chance to know her bents), I enrolled her in a dance class. What a disaster! She refused to move or even leave the wall where she stood throughout the entire class, ignoring the coaxing of both the teacher and myself. I simply didn't understand it. I thought all girls liked to dance, and because I did, I expected her to like it too. Needless to say, I removed her from class, and a few years later came to realize how she was made and what motivated her interests. I came to fall in love with the uniqueness that was my daughter exactly how God made her. It was an enjoyable adventure to witness her unfolding development, according to who she really was, and even though dancing never became a passion, eventually she chose on her own to learn some community-style dancing, much to my surprise and delight.

> *"I came to fall in love with the uniqueness that was my daughter exactly how God made her. It was an enjoyable adventure to witness her unfolding development, according to who she really was..."*

Where Change Begins

This personal example portrays what parents commonly do to their children in all areas of their development. They attempt to put on the outside a self-prescribed image of what they want their children to be like. If they want intellectual children, they might overlook the development of concrete skills, even if a child gravitates toward working with his hands. Such a child may find a lot of intellectual stimulation overwhelming and ill-fitting, just like dancing was an ill-fit for my daughter at that time of her life. If parents want their children to be good Christians, they may find a way to provide lots of Bible knowledge for their children, causing an ill fit. Knowledge is usually put on the outside like putting on a garment, instead of forming spiritual knowledge on the inside through relational growth and change so the child can truly come to know God. True change begins on the inside and works to influence the outside. It must begin with parents who are allowing God to change their particular morality [the sum of their relational practices]. What I want you to take from this message is this: *God wants to influence you toward heart-level change before you try to change your children—a top-down, inside-out approach, that provides understanding and wisdom for parenting.*

The following passage is clear about our responsibility as parents to disciple our children to the Lord. It confirms what we've been discussing about how values and faith are transferred to children, and how we as parents must be prepared for our role of discipling our children. This passage also provides the *what*—the training curriculum and the *where*—the schoolroom for our discipling activities. Here it is in both the Amplified and Message versions.

> "And **these words** which I am **commanding** you this day shall be **[first] in your own minds and hearts**: [then] you shall whet and sharpen them so as to make them penetrate, and teach and impress them diligently upon the [minds and] hearts of your children, and shall talk of them when you sit in your house and when you walk by the way, and when you lie down and when you rise up."
>
> Deuteronomy 6:6-7 AMP

> "Love God, your God, with your whole heart: love Him with all that's in you, love Him with all you've got! **Write these commandments that I've given you today on your hearts. Get them inside of you and then get them inside your children.** Talk about them wherever you are, sitting at home or walking in the street; talk about them from the time you get up in the morning to when you fall into bed at night."
>
> The Message (The bold emphasis is mine.)

1st Standard—The Father Gives the Command and Provides Parental Preparation—A Top-Down, Inside-Out Approach. God's command to parents to exercise their God-given familial authority gives us the *right* and *privilege* of influence toward God's ways. Before we can command our children for the Lord, God wants us to first allow Him to parent us. *"And these words which I am commanding you this day shall be [first] in your [own] minds and hearts; [then] you shall whet and sharpen them so as to make them penetrate..."* God commands us to disciple our children in His ways. We can't whet and sharpen truths and disciplines we haven't first received from God for ourselves and wisely worked into our own lives. If we haven't received them directly from Him, then we can be certain we aren't applying them correctly to our children, because our ways are not like His ways. We can be assured we'll get things twisted. God wants to give us *parental preparation*.

> *"Without parental preparation, we have a very limited understanding about our role as an authority figure in our children's lives."*

Without parental preparation, we have a very limited understanding of our role as an authority figure in our children's lives. Our limitations force us to choose our actions based on one of two extremes of our flesh. In license, we allow undisciplined and unchecked behavior, resulting in a measure of wild chaos, or in legalism, we impose a set of rules and a system of rewards and punishments for our children just to get them to do what we want. These actions may produce temporary and limited behavioral changes, but don't affect underlying moral character at all. With spiritual parental preparation, we can dispense with superficial "tricks of the parenting trade" that are merely forms of manipulation, and instead learn to develop Christlike relational habits, training ourselves and our children in true biblical values that result in unity, harmony, and teamwork in our family. This confirms that our preparation as parents according to God's way involves the examination of our own conscience and cooperation with the Holy Spirit toward the transformation of our own moral character first.

2nd Standard—The Father Provides the Training Curriculum—His Relational Value System. We can find this in the beginning of our passage where God says, "And these words..." The specifics for "and these words" are found in the previous verse three of the same chapter: *"That you may [reverently] fear the Lord your God, you and your son and your son's son, and keep all His statutes and His commandments which I command you all the days of your life, and that your days may be prolonged."* God is tying up together everything pertaining to how He wants us to live for Him: Christ's Law of Love—the way He wants us to think, live, and relate with Him and with others; in other words—*His relational value system.* The content of discipleship [transferring our moral values and faith] is provided through God's Law of Love at work within us as we develop Christlike character—an ability to love sacrificially, intimately, and unconditionally. And so, God's love, and not merely acquiring biblical knowledge, is our purpose, our content, and discipleship's *curriculum.* This confirms our need as parents to embrace God's ways of love in all the particulars of our relating habits so we can transfer to our children God's moral value system.

3rd Standard—The Father Provides the Schoolroom—the Heart and Mind. The heart and mind are God's workplace in our life. Parents commonly neglect the heart, while in fact, it must come first.

> *"If you acknowledge and confess with your lips that Jesus is Lord and in your **heart** believe (adhere to, trust in, and rely on the truth) that God raised Him from the dead, you will be saved. For with the **heart** a person believes (adheres to, trusts in, and relies on Christ) and so is justified (declared righteous, acceptable to God), and with the mouth he confesses (declares openly and speaks out freely his faith) and confirms [his] salvation."*
>
> Romans 10:9-10 AMP

If our efforts toward our own moral values and faith are limited to the cerebral realm, without a teachable heart being engaged, it can't influence how we relate with God and with others. If we limit our efforts toward transferring moral values and faith to our children to the cerebral realm with Bible knowledge and isolated times of teaching such as Sunday School or family devotions, we will not influence how our children relate with God and with others.

Truth must be outworked through heart-level instruction so it can impact the quality of our relationships or we risk losing the power of truth's influence, and this is why we must target the heart, both ours and our children's. Truth's purpose is to form Christlike moral character [sacrificial, intimate, and unconditionally loving relating habits], which has its beginnings in the heart, showing up in healthier relating practices, and then influencing the mind to think rightly about life. If right relating isn't happening, then truth really isn't at work at all, and we can sadly say that truth is not there. God gives us the **workplace** where the training of our children and our influence with them takes place—the same workplace God has in us. The following passages of Scripture confirm God's plan to work in our hearts.

> "But he is a Jew who is one inwardly, and **[true] circumcision is of the heart**, a spiritual and not a literal [matter]. His praise is not from men but from God."
>
> Romans 2:29 AMP

> "By that single offering, He did everything that needed to be done for everyone **who takes part in the purifying process**. The Holy Spirit confirms this: This new plan I'm making with Israel isn't going to be written on paper, isn't going to be chiseled in stone; This time **"I'm writing out the plan in them, carving it on the lining of their hearts."** He concludes, I'll forever wipe the slate clean of their sins. Once sins are taken care of for good, there's no longer any need to offer sacrifices for them."
>
> Hebrews 10:14-18 The Message

*"This time **I'm writing out the plan in them, carving it on the lining of their hearts**. I'll be their God, they'll be my people. They won't go to school to learn about me, or buy a book called God in Five Easy Lessons. They'll all get to know me firsthand, the little and the big, the small and the great. They'll get to know me by being kindly forgiven, with the slate of their sins forever wiped clean."*

Hebrews 8:10-12 The Message

A Parenting Model and Mandate

God is giving us a parenting model that includes a mandate to trust Him for both the everyday character-formation process and the outcome. This mandate can only be patterned after how God parents us. He doesn't leave us alone to have to guess at how to transfer our moral values and faith to our children. He wants us to be so parented that we will know how to disciple our children for Him. He intimately reaches our hearts and causes us to want to do His will. His involvement and leading in our lives are intimate, personal, and quite individual according to His design. His involvement meets our peculiar needs and makes us feel loved and valued. He disciplines us with kindness. He wants us to parent in this same way—His way.

So the principle lesson here is *as God parents you, so parent your children.* For the discipleship of our children to be godly and produce Christlike character, God must be in it. If He isn't, then by default, we'll be modeling a false image of the Father to our children, and they will grow up to develop a twisted view of Him and His moral values. The Lord leaves nothing to chance. He is a good Father and provider for His children who will follow Him. He does not abandon us to figure out how to live. God made sure that His concept of parenting couldn't be reduced down to nominal time in co-existence with our children or to a mere informational transference of knowledge about Him. The church is given as the Lord's helper to the family, not as a substitute. God must be allowed to influence the equation first and foremost through the parent's diligent obedience in his or her own particular moral values [relational practices].

> *"Within just months my life was changing from the inside out. I was feeling equipped to parent for the first time in my life."*

Personal Story ~ "Becoming Parented All Over Again"

When I coined the expression *"As God parents you, so parent your children"*, I had been parenting by default for about sixteen years, but only seriously engaged in experimenting with my parenting for three. So you can imagine we had a lot of bad fruit needing attention. My husband and I had been trying to stop some negative patterns of behavior that had taken hold in our oldest son a few years earlier but had remained unsuccessful in our efforts. We did all the typical things parents do when faced with a rebellious child. We exercised more authority by becoming stricter and provided more discipline in the form of punishments, which only served to drive him farther away from us. We really didn't know what else to do. It was during this strife-filled period that we began to operate in God's relational value system, but still only in general ways, since we barely understood what God was after in us. We simply had the will to obey Him and change our own ways. Since our son was already grown and leaving home, and we didn't yet possess the needed wisdom to help him, it would be a few more years when he was approaching his mid-twenties before we gained back a measure of influence with him through a restored relationship.

As we transitioned into more full-time heart-level parenting with our younger two children, God had my complete attention, and I allowed myself to "go all the way" with the work He had wanted to do in my heart all along. Within just months my life was changing from the inside out. I was feeling equipped to parent for the first time in my life. I was empowered by the Holy Spirit's work in me to completely change my parenting methods and curriculum, adopting the Lord's loving relational value system, which changed my entire focus of parenting my children. I allowed God to work in me while I worked in my children, providing instruction to them in how to connect to the Holy Spirit's influence too. My children's *hearts* [the seat of character] became my workplace [the schoolroom] in their lives just as it was God's workplace in mine.

> *"I was amazed to discover that I was becoming successful at the character formation process —to God's glory!"*

For instance, instead of addressing relational matters with a band-aid approach, which only served to pacify the immediate situation, but continued to enable my children's self-centered responses and actions, I began to see our true spiritual condition, and look beneath the surface of our family's relational problems. And so, I was continuously led by the Holy Spirit to learn how to wisely address specific relational conflicts, misunderstandings, and challenges. I was amazed to discover that I was becoming successful at the character-formation process—to God's glory! Whenever I encountered a relational challenge I didn't know how to handle, which occurred multiple times every single day, I would simply ask myself how Jesus would handle it. After all, I was fully and deeply engaged with God's parenting of me, and so I was accumulating a deep reservoir of "new" wisdom—yet untapped—to draw from. Inexperience in doing so kept me in a constant state of "fear and trembling" before the Lord, applying faith and trust that God knew what He was talking about. And so, thus the expression came to me that as God parented me, I parented my children.

The freedom, liberty, and success I experienced in God's relational way of parenting can't be overstated. Even though it took a long time for moral character to come to maturity, I didn't have to wait for years to see good fruit. I began to see positive results *right away*. I could see our family's moral character forming every single day in our relating habits and patterns. Our home's moral culture began to change dramatically for good. I never needed to read another parenting or child training book. I never again experienced concern over possible gaps in my children's education and life experiences, because I knew that if they had the most important life preparation—a strong and holy [purely loving] relational grounding—they would do well in everything else. God had become more real to me than ever, and so I learned to rest in the Lord's promises that He spoke to my heart, but more importantly, I had become more real to Him, which served to heal my soul. I became confident in the Lord and possessed tremendous assurance from Him that I was on a healthy path that would produce the desired fruit in our family. He was so faithful to me. My family became a unified team—working together to grow in true righteousness—with God's priority of love as our goal and purpose.

The Father's Invitation

Your Heavenly Father is inviting you into a relationship with Himself as the Master Teacher and Perfect Parent. He's providing you with the opportunity to develop a *living* relational model of discipleship for you to draw from for your own parenting practices. In other words, He wants to give you preparation for your parenting duties of transferring moral values and faith to your children. He wants to teach you and instruct you in His relational value system—a vital curriculum that has the power to change your whole life. You will come to understand His Moral Law of Love and learn how to walk in it.

You don't have to go anywhere special for your lessons. He has already provided you with the schoolroom where your lessons will take place—the schoolroom of your own heart first. Your heart [conscience], along with the influence of the Holy Spirit, goes with you everywhere you go. The Holy Spirit is present to instruct and guide you in every relational interaction. And finally, God not only gives you His parenting model, but also a parental mandate to learn to apply faith and trust in Him to your discipling practices; to have Him so involved in your life that you can't help but succeed in raising up your children for Him. The Lord wants to teach you how to parent as you allow Him to parent you first. Here is Christ's invitation:

> *"Are you tired? Worn out? Burned out on religion? Come to me. Get away with me and you'll recover your life. I'll show you how to take a real rest. Walk with me and work with me—watch how I do it. Learn the unforced rhythms of grace. I won't lay anything heavy or ill-fitting on you. Keep company with me and you'll learn to live freely and lightly."*
> Matthew 11:28 The Message

Look at this clear instruction! Your first lesson from God is to not lay anything heavy or ill-fitting on your children as I did to my precious daughter with regard to dancing. God won't do this to us, because He made each of us unique for a particular purpose. The discovery of that purpose is given to each one personally, and with heart-level preparation, our children have a chance of learning what they were made for. God wants to address the heart—your heart and your children's hearts.

Don't believe the lie that only the Holy Spirit can have access to another's heart. The lie will only serve to excuse you from your God-given parental responsibility. If you don't have the hearts of your children, don't expect God to have them. Remember God's mandate and model! He will become as intimately involved with you as you allow Him to be, and through the Holy Spirit in you, you'll be able to be intimately involved with your children.

Perhaps you've heard this adaptation of a well-known inspiring quote, a further reminder of where all change must begin: *God grant me the serenity to accept the people I cannot change, the courage to change the one I can, and the wisdom to know it's me.* My children are so glad I allowed the Lord to change me. To God be the glory for the great things He has done!

Remember—*As God parents you, so parent your children.*

Testimonies

Tim and **Barbie Poling** describe their parenting model before they understood how to exercise heart-level influence with their children. They describe the fruit of their prior parenting model in themselves and their children, and how that impacted their relationships with them.

> *Tim ~ By default, I held the opinion that children must be obedient and quiet. I was overly harsh, and I displayed my displeasure toward them by being rough in handling them and speaking to them as if they were stupid. I had very little interest in the children's interests, because their interests were very different from my own, and I really didn't care about the subjects they were interested in. My self-image was important to me so if I thought my children were making me look badly, I would get angry and emotionally punish them. As a result, my children didn't come to me with their interests or concerns, and they were afraid of me, which created distance in our relationships even though they were obedient.*

> "My oldest son especially was concerning me. He had developed a habit of unashamed lying about his responsibilities, and short angry outbursts at his siblings that were getting more frequent rather than less." ~ Barbie

> *Barbie ~ My parenting produced children who were respectful of adults, quickly obedient, and hard workers. The relational*

*fruit, however, began to become **apparent** as my children got to be ten or eleven years old. I noticed them beginning to resist me in subtle ways. They seemed to be becoming more independent, but not in a way that was a blessing. They seemed somehow closed off from me in a measure. My oldest son especially was concerning me. He had developed a habit of unashamed lying about his responsibilities, and short angry outbursts at his siblings that were getting more frequent rather than less. He gave me the feeling that he was hiding something from me. My oldest children became less affectionate toward me. I didn't know what to do about these concerns.*

8 Challenging Ideas and Corresponding Sobering Realities

Challenging Idea #1 ~ *Most Christian parents don't know what moral and spiritual training consists of and are leaving it to chance.*

Sobering Reality #1 ~ *You are being told on by your own relational fruit, but the hope is that God wants to empower you to change your fruit.*

Challenging Idea #2 ~ *Morality is the heart-level quality of how people relate with each other, defining character as the sum of our relational habits.*

Sobering Reality #2 ~ *The state of your relationships defines your character and reflects your true spiritual condition. You are your children's character education.*

Challenging Idea #3 ~ *It's impossible to transfer moral values in broad generalities that are unrelational. They are successfully instilled only by addressing the particulars of your family's heart-level relating habits and patterns.*

Sobering Reality #3 ~ *A biblical morality is clearly defined in all of its relational particulars.*

Challenging Idea #4 ~ True spiritual growth occurs when we bring our particular morality in line with Christ's Law of Love, making our instruction in moral rectitude completely relational.

Sobering Reality #4 ~ Love's evidence [God's standard for moral fruit] is seen in the sacrificial quality of the heart-level attitudes, intentions, and motivations of your relating practices.

Challenging Idea #5 ~ Relational immorality is sin, and sin—simply stated—is a self-centered failure to love, and falling short of love is immoral in God's eyes, even wicked and evil.

Sobering Reality #5 ~ Heart attitudes, intentions, and motivations toward others tell the truth about the quality of your morality.

Challenging Idea #6 ~ God gives us the Law of Love, a powerful tool to accomplish two practical purposes—to know ourselves and to know Him.

Sobering Reality #6 ~ Conscience is the most sacred of all your personal property.

Challenging Idea #7 ~ *God wants to influence you toward heart-level change before you try to change your children—a top-down, inside-out approach that provides understanding and wisdom for parenting.*

Sobering Reality #7 ~ *As God parents you, so parent your children.*

Chapter 8

The Price to Form Moral Character

~ Challenging Idea and Sobering Reality #8 ~
"The price to form moral character is a narrow physical environment in an atmosphere consistent with God's ways of love."
~ Relational character training adds time to your every duty and every duty ought to stop for character training.

We need to weigh in on the cost factor to form moral character. There is a reality we simply need to acknowledge as individuals and as the church. There is a price to pay to form our children's moral character. It is the same price that forms our own. In *The Death of Character,* Hunter observed that the reality of the way in which character is successfully passed on to children requires that moral instruction be *particular* instead of *general* and inclusive. Moral education has its most enduring effects on young people when their relational and social world (family life, school, and church community) shares a defined moral culture that is mutually reinforcing. He found that among devout Catholic and Jewish communities, when morality is being taught alongside academic education and reinforced by the family and the whole community, there is success with the forming of moral character. He also found, however, that if certain people didn't like what was being taught, they were welcome to leave. There is no effort made to be inclusive like there is in secular institutions and most Christian churches.

Parents of Influence

We must learn how to oversee our children's attitudes, intentions, and motivations as they are outworked in their relationships, and choose educational and religious influences that don't undermine these efforts but actually reinforce them. The implications are quite clear. In order to become parents who influence our children's moral values and faith at the heart level, we must first become parented at the heart level, and it requires us to be present to our children as they are relating with others. We must agree to be positioned for this work so we can become more responsible in forming our children's *particular* moral character [the sum of their relational habits].

This presents a challenge to parents who have structured their lives according to society's ways of fragmenting the family. If your family already has a lifestyle that can accommodate one parent at home, then the challenge to you is only in your relational priorities and lifestyle activities. However, if your family is split up in several directions almost every day, the logistical challenges to you will need some time to work out before you can be positioned for an efficient work that is not undermined at every turn.

My Story ~ "Staking My Claim"

When my husband made the decision and convinced me that we needed to homeschool our family, I had no idea at the time that God was involved in our decision. However, Jim wanted to reclaim our children, and so we staked a claim in the land of our own lives. We knew our decision was permanent and we would somehow figure things out.

Many have yet to claim their family for the Lord even though they have physical possession of their children at home. They may not know how to cooperate with the work God wants to do in their family. It took me about six years for the Lord to get Egypt (the world's educational value system) completely out of me. It didn't happen all at once, but as I gradually adopted more of the Lord's values, the more I invested in my children's character (their true education). This was a very personal and meaningful process that formed deep bonds in our family relationships, causing the stake to be driven deeper into the ground of our lives. Our investment would overflow into every area of our family's life and God would eventually use our family to meet the real needs of other families.

If you're one of those who have come out of Egypt but have not yet allowed the Lord to remove the values of Egypt from your heart, why not stake a claim right now for the souls of your children?

My Story ~ "Forming My Family's Morality"

I want to share how my own family's morality was formed after we were born again [when we trusted Christ's salvation and began to cooperate with the work of His influence in our hearts]. Since my husband and I educated and discipled our children at home, their moral instruction became very particular. As we submitted more of our own ways to the Lord, this produced the fruit of moral integrity in our relationships, and thus true character formation and true righteousness—right-standing with God—in our spiritual lives. Our family's morality was formed through a committed process in the Lord of consistently dealing with specific relational problems and challenges, according to the Law of Love.

> *"We created a relational environment where all the activity of our home was organized around the development of healthy relationships between family members."*

In the earlier years when the restructuring of how we related with each other was taking place, we narrowed our family's lifestyle environment to make possible the processes needed for regular and consistent instruction to bring about transformation. We created a relational environment where all the activity of our home was organized around the development of healthy relationships between family members. All potential activities outside the home were evaluated as to how they would nurture our internal family relationships, and for the best timing any desired activity ought to be included in our lives. Regular duties and activities paused long enough to deal with relational conflicts that arose throughout the day.

The Lord was good to lead us in this process and gave us wisdom for how much narrowing of our environment was needed. We never isolated our family, but only insulated it enough to create a culture conducive to training that could not be undermined at every turn. The Lord affirmed to us many times we were on the right path. His Word provided another confirmation that will be helpful to you as well. It's found in Proverbs.

> "Train up a child in the way he should go [and in keeping with his individual gift or bent], and when he is old he will not depart from it."
>
> Proverbs 22:6 AMP

The Price For Moral Character

This passage is richly loaded, but we're going to limit our examination of it to just the word "train."

> TRAIN—In a character sense, "to train" is used in conjunction with the word "sober"—the cultivation of sound judgment and prudence; to cause to be of sound mind.

Is there a serious parent who doesn't want their children to develop a disciplined mind that thinks straight about truth? It is my belief that most people do want what is best for their families, but sadly, we fail to understand what it takes to actually cultivate this sort of mature Christlike character. If we ever happen to find out what our commitment to our responsibilities should be, many, like the rich young ruler who walked away from Christ after learning the price of following Him, would turn their backs in self-centered defeat unwilling to give up the lifestyle they're living that prevents them from consistently addressing the relational behavior of their children. In *The Death of Character,* Hunter tells how the church is failing in the character-formation department. In fact, he says that character is all but dead in our church and nation because we are simply not willing to pay the price for the formation of moral character.

> *"We want character but without conviction; we want strong morality but without the emotional burden of guilt or shame; we want virtue but without particular moral justifications that invariably offend; we want good without having to name evil; we want decency without the authority to insist upon it; we want moral community without any limitations to personal freedom. In short, we want what we cannot possibly have on the terms that we want it."*

But for those of us who are willing to pay such a price for our children's sake, God gives us a plan, and even paints a bit of a picture for us so we can see how it works.

A Narrow Environment for Training

Here's more on the word "train." The primary meaning of "train" will help us to understand the price God is asking parents to pay in order to cultivate sound moral judgment and wisdom in our children's character [relational practices].

> TRAIN — *"to narrow" in order to dedicate for a specific process of discipline.*

When I first came across this definition in my personal studies, I asked the Lord, to narrow what? The examples given within the definition imply a choking of life or cutting off; a restricting of something. For instance, in gardening, "train" is to direct and form to a wall or espalier. Forming to a trellis requires pruning the plant or tree so it will be shaped properly for growth. This pruning process brings a narrowing to the plant's environment so it can't just go in any old direction, but it will grow in the gardener's desired direction. Jesus' way of training us is also narrow so we'll grow in the proper direction, according to His ways and purposes. He confirms this in His own words.

> *"Enter through the narrow gate; for wide is the gate and spacious and broad is the way that leads away to destruction, and many are those who are entering through it. But the gate is narrow (contracted by pressure) and the way is straitened and compressed that leads away to life, and few are those who find it."*
>
> Matthew 7:13-14 AMP

Training brings a very real pressure on our lives to conform and compress to a straight path in moral character formation. This training in appropriate relational disciplines is for our good success, for it will conform us to Christlikeness, healing our primary relationships, and making us fit for every good use.

Two Applications for the Principle of Narrowing

I can see two possibilities for applying the principle of narrowing for the purposes of developing more spiritual influence with our children, which will result in the formation of our family's moral character.

> ***1.) Narrow Our Focus and Efforts***—*It's imperative for us as parents to narrow our focus and efforts sufficiently in order to facilitate deep and powerful training of moral character,*

which can only be accomplished through relationships between family members that are allowed to become intimate and real [truthful and authentic]. We cannot be haphazard, but must be intentional in this endeavor, willingly setting all the priorities of our lives in order so we can get to work on the relationships within our family. We need to learn how to deeply identify and understand what is wrong in our relating habits, and how to change them.

2.) Narrow Our Physical Environment—*It's also imperative that we narrow our physical environment enough to accomplish this objective. Narrowing our environment positions us to hear from God and to receive His instruction. We are saying that we are now available to His work. Just think about this: tighter boundaries for living are common for those who are committing their lives to special training, such as with military basic training or sports/skill training. This principle can be seen at work all throughout our society—in our educational institutions where any equipping endeavor takes place. We even provide our children with basic academic skills within a tightly constrained environment almost to the point of overkill. And yet, we leave moral character formation—their whole-life preparation—to chance.*

It's sad that the most important equipping of all, our relational moral character and that of our children, doesn't even begin to be addressed with a formal plan to ensure that it actually happens. The implications are clear and significant. We really have been experiencing the death of moral character in our world today. There truly does appear to be a wholesale abandonment of parental responsibility, at least according to God's standards of Love. We want the fruit without having to engage in the process. We want our children's hearts to be influenced by us, but we don't want to narrow our efforts to accomplish this wonderful end. We are missing out on so much joy and fulfillment when we deny ourselves of our God-given responsibilities. Perhaps one of the hardest lessons we have to learn as a church is this: the price to form moral character is a narrow physical environment in an atmosphere consistent with God's ways of loving accountability between people who walk in humility and truth-telling.

Allow the Home to Do the Work only the Home Can Do ~ What It Should Look Like

God's work begins in your home where you set the standards for relational moral character development, and are responsible to provide a caring watchfulness over all aspects of your children's maturation. You allow only the regular influence of other adults who are interested to support such an effort, such as a school with an emphasis on developing character or a church where parental authority and responsibility are not undermined, and in fact, are encouraged and supported.

> *"Your family's moral culture becomes very practical and particular in all relational matters, providing specific explanations for the 'whys' of developing certain relating habits, for instance, 'why we do and say what we do and say.'"*

In such an environment, while intellectual and academic virtues are viewed as very important, they submit to the higher-order goals of forming relational moral character in all your family relationships. Your family's moral culture becomes very practical and particular in all relational matters, providing specific explanations for the "whys" of developing certain relating habits, for instance, "why we do and say what we do and say." As you allow your home to do the work only the home can do, the particulars of your family's moral culture develop. Right relating habits become authoritative and binding on individual conscience and family life, resulting in Christlike character.

To prepare our environment for relational growth, that integrates Christlike character education into every aspect of home life, we really need a plan, for it is not only a narrowed environment the family needs, but it must be accompanied by the correct spiritual atmosphere if Christlike objectives are to be accomplished. This is why beginning with parents is a must. The correct spiritual atmosphere must come from you, the parent, through the work you allow the Holy Spirit to do in your heart, bringing you into moral rectitude [a holy quality of morality]. God is relational and He wants to relate with you. The progression of your sanctification [inner growth toward Christlikeness] and that of your children is a team effort, depending upon what you do as well as what God does for you and in you.

Another Price to Form Moral Character ~ Humility and Truth-Telling that Opens Up Relationships

Giving yourself to the holy [purely loving] endeavor of forming Christlike character in your family is only one price you pay. Another cost is the accountability that truth-telling between spouses entails. Without humble honesty between spouses, you will limit your own spiritual growth. Allow yourself to receive from a human agency so you can get to the bottom of your own fleshly relational habits and learn how to receive the grace and unconditional love your spouse has to offer you. Married couples have the best opportunity for relational intimacy and trust building, and to experience God's amazing grace through another human being. Begin by allowing your spouse to speak into your life, and hear how some of your actions make them feel. He or she knows you best. Choose to build trust with each other so honest and open, loving communication can take place that will help you become free of relating strongholds of which you are unaware. Instead of covering up the truth in self-protection, choose to tell the truth about yourself and your actions so you can disarm the enemy's lies in your life. Practice addressing actual behavioral practices in real time, taking the time needed for appropriate communications so understanding can grow between family members, resulting in reconciliation.

On the following page is a scriptural model for the family home atmosphere parents can use as a goal while bringing themselves and their children under the discipline and training of the Lord. It presents many distinguishing features of a healthy spiritual environment. Won't you begin to allow your home to do the work only your home can do?

A Merciful Reminder—Character training adds time to your every duty and every duty ought to stop for character training.

Editor's Note: *In the next chapter, Barbie Poling tells about the Ministry of Reconciliation through her personal testimony of how the Lord brought miracles to her family, beginning with her mother who was in an advanced stage of Alzheimer's.*

A Scriptural Goal for the Family Home Atmosphere

Colossians 3:12-17

12) "Clothe yourselves therefore, as God's own chosen ones (His own picked representatives), [who are] purified and holy and well-beloved [by God Himself, by putting on behavior marked by] tenderhearted pity and mercy, kind feeling, a lowly opinion of yourselves, gentle ways, [and] patience [which is tireless and long-suffering, and has the power to endure whatever comes, with good temper]."

13) "Be gentle and forbearing with one another, and if one has a difference (a grievance or complaint) against another, readily pardoning each other; even as the Lord has [freely] forgiven you, so must you also [forgive]."

14) "And above all these [put on] love and enfold yourselves with the bond of perfectness [which binds everything together completely in ideal harmony]."

15) "And let the peace (soul harmony which comes) from Christ rule (act as umpire continually) in your hearts [deciding and settling with finality all questions that arise in your minds, in that peaceful state] to which as [members of Christ's] one body you were also called [to live]. And be thankful (appreciative), [giving praise to God always]."

16) "Let the word [spoken by] Christ (the Messiah) have its home [in your hearts and minds] and dwell in you in [all its] richness, as you teach and admonish and train one another in all insight and intelligence and wisdom [in spiritual things, and as you sing] psalms and hymns and spiritual songs, making melody to God with [His] grace in your hearts."

17) "And whatever you do [no matter what it is] in word or deed, do everything in the name of the Lord Jesus and in [dependence upon] His Person, giving praise to God the Father through Him."

Philippians 1:9-11

Verse 9) "This I pray for you that your love may abound yet more and more and extend to its fullest development in knowledge and all keen insight [that your love may display itself in greater depth of acquaintance and more comprehensive discernment]."

10) "So that you may surely learn to sense what is vital, and approve and prize what is excellent and of real value [recognizing the highest and the best, and distinguishing the moral differences], and that you may be untainted and pure and unerring and blameless [so that with hearts sincere and certain and unsullied, you may approach] the day of Christ [not stumbling nor causing others to stumble]."

11) "May you abound in and be filled with the fruits of righteousness (of right standing with God and right doing) which come through Jesus Christ the Anointed One), to the honor and praise of God [that His glory may be both manifested and recognized]."

Testimonies

Barbie describes how she narrowed her focus and environment when beginning to practice heart-level parenting, and the good fruit that resulted.

> *The first narrowing of our environment came as I stopped reaching out toward getting together with my friends and their children. Marilyn asked me multiple times if I thought I needed so many friends or why I had so many friends. I just didn't have an answer. I had friends because friends were fun to hang out with. As I stopped pursuing my friends, I found there was not really anyone pursuing me back except some quite needy people that I knew I did not have the ability to help. My awareness of my inability to help others had been rapidly increasing since beginning to learn heart-level parenting.*

> "My awareness of my inability to help others had been rapidly increasing since beginning to learn heart-level parenting." ~ Barbie

> *With the absence of "friends" and their children in our lives, we became much more home focused. I began to have a strong desire to be led by the Holy Spirit in all areas of my life so I focused on some word studies the Lord had led me to, and learning to love specifically my mom who was living with us. I focused on the kid's hearts toward their gramma and then toward each other.*

Later I began to understand the connection between peer influence and developing false personality in my children. At that time we were very involved in a homeschool band and choir. When the year ended, I pulled my kids out of the program. I encouraged them to pursue music at home together with each other and alone where there were no peers or program expectations to influence them. As they worked together on music, their relationships and appreciation for each other grew stronger, and attitudes surfaced that we were able to confront and deal with. The kids became free to discover their own interest in the music that was coming from what God had put within them. Some of their instruments were abandoned. Other musical interests surfaced. We hired a voice teacher to come to our home and we began to sing together as a family choir. We all realized how much our involvement in the music program was actually holding us back musically! We also were able to see how much the program and the peers were influencing the kids toward things that were not really their interests. Apart from the program, the kids were free from unproductive outside influences to become who God made them to be.

8 Challenging Ideas and Corresponding Sobering Realities

Challenging Idea #1 ~ *Most Christian parents don't know what moral and spiritual training consists of and are leaving it to chance.*

Sobering Reality #1 ~ *You are being told on by your own relational fruit, but the hope is that God wants to empower you to change your fruit.*

Challenging Idea #2 ~ *Morality is the heart-level quality of how people relate with each other, defining character as the sum of our relational habits.*

Sobering Reality #2 ~ *The state of your relationships defines your character and reflects your true spiritual condition. You are your children's character education.*

Challenging Idea #3 ~ *It's impossible to transfer moral values in broad generalities that are unrelational. They are successfully instilled only by addressing the particulars of your family's heart-level relating habits and patterns.*

Sobering Reality #3 ~ *A biblical morality is clearly defined in all of its relational particulars.*

Challenging Idea #4 *~ True spiritual growth occurs when we bring our particular morality in line with Christ's Law of Love, making our instruction in moral rectitude completely relational.*

Sobering Reality #4 *~ Love's evidence [God's standard for moral fruit] is seen in the sacrificial quality of the heart-level attitudes, intentions, and motivations of your relating practices.*

Challenging Idea #5 *~ Relational immorality is sin, and sin—simply stated—is a self-centered failure to love, and falling short of love is immoral in God's eyes, even wicked and evil.*

Sobering Reality #5 *~ Heart attitudes, intentions, and motivations toward others tell the truth about the quality of your morality.*

Challenging Idea #6 *~ God gives us the Law of Love, a powerful tool to accomplish two practical purposes—to know ourselves and to know Him.*

Sobering Reality #6 *~ Conscience is the most sacred of all your personal property.*

Challenging Idea #7 *~ God wants to influence you toward heart-level change before you try to change your children—a top-down, inside-out approach that provides understanding and wisdom for parenting.*

Sobering Reality #7 *~ As God parents you, so parent your children.*

Challenging Idea #8 *~ The price to form moral character is a narrow physical environment in an atmosphere consistent with God's ways of love.*

Sobering Reality #8 *~ Relational character training adds time to your every duty, and every duty ought to stop for character training.*

Chapter 9

The Ministry of Reconciliation

~ Ellen's Story as Told by Her Daughter, Barbie Poling

Portions of this story were spoken by Barbie Poling at the memorial service for her mother, Ellen Spencer Connett.

Blessed by My Mom

My mom's life was a blessing to me in many ways, beginning at my birth when she had a severe case of thrombophlebitis, which resulted in emergency surgery that left many inch-long scars up and down both of her legs. As I cared for her over the last few years, each day I saw those scars and was reminded of the sacrifice she made to bring me into this world.

I'm blessed that my mom answered my many questions as a child. "Why are we going so slow? Why did they hang those flowers up there? Why are there gold plaques at the bottom of some of the big stained-glass windows?

Why is nine cents too expensive for watermelon?" I can't ever remember a time that she was bothered by my questions or failed to answer them in one form or another.

I'm blessed that my mom passed on to me a love of laughter. I remember how our drama teacher at the high school would invite her to attend all the plays' performances for free just so that the audience would be inspired to laugh when hearing her infectious and loud laughter. My mom had a love for clever humor, and in my life, I continue to be blessed by a good bout of hearty laughter.

I'm thankful that my mom passed on to me a love of music. I remember when I began to have the desire to play the piano my mom gave me basic theory lessons as I shouted out from the living room piano, "What does a little '7' up in the air and little 'SUS' mean?" She would shout back from the kitchen, "It means to raise the third to the fourth and add the seventh to it."

I'm blessed that my mom stayed married to my dad until death parted them, and that I wasn't raised in a divorce situation.

> *"I'm writing these things of the past in order to share the need that my mom had for the awesome reconciliation that she experienced in the last few years of her life."*

I'm blessed that my mom raised me in the knowledge of God, the belief that He answers prayer, and that our concerns are never too small for Him. I'm blessed that my mom raised me in the church and taught me by example that church is more than just an activity to attend once a week. She showed me that we need to be involved in the ministry of the church. My mom loved to teach and explain things in an easy-to-understand way. I'm thankful that she passed that on to me because I love doing that too. My mom had a strong desire to understand and help people which was expressed through her interest in psychology, through speech therapy, and through developing her skill at listening and asking thought-provoking questions. I am also very interested in helping and understanding people.

But the biggest blessing of all my life was having the privilege of taking care of my mom in my home for the last five years of her life. Her final years are characterized by an awesome testimony of reconciliation. This is the story I want to tell you.

In order to tell my mom's testimony of reconciliation, I also need to give you a before and after picture of the events that transpired. My mom's reconciliation changed her life in dramatic ways and in turn, changed my life and the lives of my family.

As I'm telling this story you may feel as though I'm "airing dirty laundry" or exposing family secrets that are better kept secret. You may be thinking that I wouldn't say them if my mom knew. But let me assure you and comfort you. I have told this story multiple times with my mom by my side as I have given this testimony of reconciliation. She was eager to hear me tell it and she would interject with, "Oh, yes! That's right! It's all true!" Even just days before her death, I was recounting this testimony to someone who was visiting. My mom could barely speak anymore at that time, and she took a hold of my hand while I was talking. I turned to see what she needed, but all she wanted was to say to me, "Keep going", so I will keep going and telling this story.

My Mom's Background

My mom was heavily involved in church activity and various forms of ministry throughout her adult life. I always had the impression that our family was thought of in our church as a model Christian family and yet, the Christianity that my mom lived and taught didn't run deep enough to touch the core of her being where life-long hurt, alienation, relational separation, and ill-will pervaded.

Through the circumstances that my mom chose during my childhood, I emerged into my young adult years experiencing a lack of affection and indifference from my mom in her relationship with me. I had for the most part developed my life—that is my friendships, my activities, and interests—essentially without her. While she attended some of the events of my life and she was present at home in the evenings, she was not present to my heart, or to my thoughts, or to my emotions and feelings, because there was emotional separation and indifference between us.

As I went off to college, the distance and alienation in my mom's relationship with me only grew. I was busy with school and new friends and I didn't think much about my relationship with her until I was living in a spare room with a family whose phone I shared. One day the wife of the family asked me, "Why doesn't your mom ever want to talk to you on the phone? Why is your dad the only one who calls you?" I knew that it wasn't that she just didn't like talking on the phone, because she talked to many people on the phone for long periods of time, so I tried to explain to her the circumstances of my life that resulted in the indifference and this separation of relationship between my mom and me.

My Mom's Need for Reconciliation

I'm writing these things of the past in order to share the need that my mom had for the awesome reconciliation that she experienced in the last few years of her life. I'm giving you the "before" picture. Her need for reconciliation was visible and apparent in the way she related to me, and the way that I learned from her to relate in return. To most people who knew our family, that need was not visible because it existed within her closest relationships—those with her spouse and children.

Reconciliation ~ A Definition

My mom's story is the message of reconciliation that 2 Corinthians chapter 5 speaks of.

> *"But all things are from God, Who through Jesus Christ reconciled us to Himself [received us into favor, brought us into harmony with Himself] and gave to us the ministry of reconciliation [that by word and deed we might aim to bring others into harmony with Him]. It was God [personally present] in*

Christ, reconciling and restoring the world to favor with Himself, not counting up and holding against [men] their trespasses [but cancelling them], and committing to us the message of reconciliation (of the restoration to favor)."

2 Corinthians 5:18-19

The dictionary definition of reconciliation says: To lead or draw someone back toward affection, favor, and goodwill; to call back into union and friendship the affections which have been alienated; to restore to friendship or favor after estrangement; as, to reconcile parties that have been at variance. This definition of reconciliation speaks of the conditions that signify that someone is in need of reconciliation. It says these conditions include:

- Alienation, which is to be withdrawing in affection and indifference existing between people.

- Estrangement, which means to keep yourself or another at a distance or to be mentally absent or separate in relationships.

- Parties that have been at variance, which is about differences, disputes, controversies, disagreements, dissension, discord, and bad feelings, such as ill will, fault-finding, and even hatred between people.

Consider Your Own Close Relationships

It leads us to consider our close relationships, which are those of our family. Is there alienation, distance, lack of affection, withholding of affection, or mental or emotional separateness? These are the symptoms of a need for reconciliation, even if these conditions have lasted for years and it seems like they're just the way it is. Just as Marilyn's *challenging idea #2* says, "Morality is the heart-level quality of how people relate with each other, defining character as the sum of our relational habits...The state of your relationships defines your character and reflects your true spiritual condition."

These relational behaviors defined my mom's relationship with me and revealed her need to be reconciled. We are all able, like my mom was, to put a polite and socially acceptable personality on top of these symptoms for relating with those outside the family, but those who live or have lived with each one of us experience our true habitual relational behaviors—our moral character.

> *"...Leads us to consider our close relationships, which are those of our family. Is there alienation, distance, lack of affection, withholding of affection, mental or emotional separateness? These are the symptoms of a need for reconciliation..."*

I married and had children and lived in various locations across the states, and at that time I saw my mom only two or three times a year or less. As Alzheimer's disease began taking its toll on my mom's mind, she slowly lost the ability to keep up the polite, socially acceptable appearance that she had once had, and her relational distance and alienation became more exposed. The ill will and anger that had always been deep in her heart began to emerge more regularly. In her visits with my family, she remained mostly silent, inwardly focused, and often scowling. She did not interact with or make eye contact with me, my husband, or my children. She did not want to hold my babies or smile, talk, and play with my children. As time passed, the expression of her anger and ill will grew. During her visits she began to occasionally lash out at my children, roughly grabbing and shaking them in order to harshly rebuke them for insignificant or unknown things. She treated them like enemies who needed to be suspiciously watched and aggressively handled.

By the time my parents came to live with me in 2004, my children had learned in their fear of her to keep their distance. She was demanding, ungrateful, resentful, harsh, angry, and mean. They had never known her to be gentle, kind, or friendly or to laugh, smile and talk with them. They had never heard her use their names. My children ignored her and vacated whatever part of the house she was in. They attempted to serve her when I directed them because by that time there were many things that she could not do for herself, but their service was at the least a dreadful duty and sometimes a fearful and frustrating experience. She ignored us all except to scold or demand. She referred to us as, "that noisy family that lives upstairs."

My Dad Dies

In January 2005, my dad passed away. His passing left me with full care and responsibility for my mom. Because of Alzheimer's disease, she couldn't be left alone; she was always with us. Her sour presence permeated our whole life and our collective feelings for her took on their own sour and oppressive nature.

In many respects, my mom was very much like a young child. She needed me to make all her decisions for her, take care of her clothing needs, prepare all her food, direct all her activities, carry all her responsibilities, and also, just like a child, she had a set of attitudes, intentions, and motivations that in her case negatively affected the way she habitually related with everyone around her. Practically speaking, my mom needed me to parent her, and I was doing so in all aspects of her life except for the workings of her heart (her attitudes, intentions, and motivations). At that time I didn't even know that was something to do, even with my own children.

I believe that is the case with many parents. We know how to meet our children's needs in so many physical and practical areas of their lives, but we're neglecting the deepest needs of their hearts, mostly out of our own ignorance, and also because we have never had the experience of another working in our own hearts in the way that we need. We don't actually know what we're aiming for or that we need to aim for it at all. We see the effects of heart-level activity in the troublesome relational practices of our family, such as bickering, isolation, insatiable desire for peers or shyness and fear, but we're powerless to bring change at the heart level. Like Marilyn's *challenging idea #1* says, *"Most Christian parents don't know what moral and spiritual training consists of and are leaving it to chance...You are being told on by your own relational fruit."* The fruit of Gramma's relationship with us, and ours with her displayed our need for reconciliation.

Marilyn Comes Over ~ February 2006

I invited Marilyn Howshall to come over and meet my family. As we visited, she observed the oppressive sourness in our home atmosphere—how Gramma ignored us, and we ignored her, and we were all unhappy.

Later, she asked if she could come back and pray with my mom. She told me that while the disease had robbed my mom of her mind, the difficulties in our relationship were coming not from her mind, but from her spirit, which was in need of reconciliation. I didn't understand it much, but I was willing to let her pray with my mom if she wanted to.

Through Marilyn's cooperation with the Holy Spirit's instruction, miracles began to happen right away. Marilyn led my mom to see her need for repentance to me. She was working in my mom's heart, targeting the attitudes she held toward me and appealing to her conscience and her need to repent of past sins against me that she could not even remember. Marilyn was bringing my mom to focus on the hurt she had caused and helping her to let go of self-focus. The miraculous part was that my mom's memory was about 10-20 seconds long at that time. She was incapable of having a conversation or tracking a line of thought, but for this and subsequent conversations, my mom became lucid and aware for relatively long spans of time—up to an hour and a half at a time!

> "The change in my mom was shockingly instant."

When Marilyn came to pray and talk with her the second time, she called me in after a bit saying, "Your mom has something to say to you." As I walked into the room my mom was weeping. She held out her hands toward me. I took her hands and she looked into my eyes and said, "I'm sooo sorry, will you please forgive me?" With tears, I told her I did forgive her. We sat for a bit there and she did not let go of my hand or stop looking at me. She kept repeating to Marilyn, "This is my daughter, Barbara." I was so amazed that she knew my name and that she looked into my eyes, and it melted me that she wanted to hold my hand. The reconciliation had begun.

The change in my mom was shockingly instant. During the next days, she began to be grateful for the things that were being done for her and she started saying, "Please" when she wanted something. Here are a few other miraculous things I noted in my journal at the time.

Thursday, Feb 9, 2006—While at the children's choir rehearsal, I seated Gramma over on the left side of the auditorium as usual, and then I went to sit with the kids on the right side. A few minutes later, she came walking over with her walker to where I was. I asked her where she was going and she said, "I was looking for you because I wanted to sit with you."

Saturday, Feb 11, 2006—Gramma watched my husband, Tim, clean a window and then told him he was doing a great job. She then walked into the kitchen and said to me, "I just wanted to tell you how much I appreciate you...and don't worry about me, I've already had my breakfast." Both Tim and I stared at each other in such delighted shock. She hadn't had her breakfast, but just days ago she would have been pounding on the arms of her chair angry that she didn't have anything to eat.

Monday, Feb 13, 2006—Gramma watched my son, Phillip, doing some work and she repeated over and over, "He's doing such a nice job! He's working so hard!" She wanted to know his name and she rehearsed it several times. When he came close by, she said, "Phillip! You've done such a nice job!" Phillip was just amazed.

I wrote these things and many more like them in my journal because they were so shocking and amazing to us. The alienation, indifference, and emotional separation were melting away. Then we knew! It was not the *disease* that was causing her to behave so badly. It was the disease that *uncovered* what had been there in her heart all along.

My mom's radical change never went away. It wasn't momentary or short-lived. Her heart—the condition of her spirit—changed. I have seen this happen in many lives now—radical, swift, and lasting change in the whole demeanor of my children, my husband, and now in others to whom I've had the privilege of ministering, and it overflows to their husbands and children. It's the result of heart-level repentance and reconciliation.

My Turn to Minister

After this initial heart-level communication between Marilyn and my mom, it wasn't long before Marilyn told me that her intention was that I begin to minister to my mom's needs the way she had begun to do, and now it was my turn to have my heart worked on! I didn't want to minister to my mom, and I didn't really even know what that meant. All I knew was that I didn't want to treat my mom the way I had seen Marilyn doing in front of me in my own home. I didn't want to shower her with verbal and physical affection, look into her eyes and help her to pray even though I easily did all these things with my children.

I had to wrestle with my attitudes, intentions, and motivations toward my mom. I quickly and truthfully labeled my thought process, (reasons for my lack of desire and emotional distance toward my mom) as unloving and evil, and I began to obey my conscience in everything I thought about doing for my mom (following Marilyn's example) with chosen willingness and eagerness. Marilyn's *challenging idea #5* says, *"Relational immorality is sin, and sin—simply stated—is a self-centered failure to love...Heart attitudes, intentions, and motivations toward others tell the truth about the quality of your morality."* I was being faced with my own moral character and my lack of love for my mom.

No Poof! But Cooperation

As my mom went through the beginnings of all these miraculous changes, I began to feel like God had suddenly decided to do a miracle in my mom. Marilyn helped me to see that my thinking about that was twisted and wrong. God had always wanted to do this work in my mom; He was just waiting for someone to cooperate with Him in it. Marilyn helped me to understand that God didn't just come into my mom's life and "Poof!!" change things. Many believers wait for God to do such things, but He is waiting for us to cooperate in a relationship with Him. In my mom's life, Marilyn was the available and yielded vessel who obeyed the promptings of the Holy Spirit's personal leading in her life, which brought these changes into the reality that God had always wanted for my mom.

> *"Marilyn's truth-telling opened my eyes to understand there was much more that God wanted to do in my mom's life, and if I would seek Him and obey, I would see those things happen too."*

Marilyn's truth-telling opened my eyes to understand that there was much more that God wanted to do in my mom's life, and if I would seek Him and obey, I would see those things happen too. I began to tune in to what God wanted to do in my mom's life. I began to ask what He wanted and to expect answers. In this way, I received very specific actions to take with and for my mom.

Over the next few weeks, the Lord helped me to know how to talk and pray with my mom over the issues of her life that had influenced the way she was relating with us. My mom and I had many conversations in which she miraculously became free from the effects of Alzheimer's disease and was able to have coherent conversations. I was so shocked by her ability to carry a full conversation that I wrote down nearly everything she was saying. I have been tempted to write her every word here, but it would just be too long.

In the next week, I talked and prayed with my mom about her resentment against God for making her a girl. She repented and asked God's forgiveness. Soon she began to identify all my kids by name, including my girls. We were all so amazed to hear her using the girls' names because she had not done that before. Here are a couple of the entries I made in my journal.

February 15, 2006

- This morning Josiah volunteered to give Gramma a hug. She hugged him really tight and repeatedly rehearsed his name.

- The children gathered around Gramma's chair laughing and playing with some headband heart-bobbers. Gramma laughed the most. Then the kids put the bobbers on her head and she became very silly by making faces and laughing and shaking the bobbers.

Ministry to My Children

My repentance of heart and behavior toward my mom quickly led to my ability to see what needed to happen in the hearts of my children as well. It was like a veil had lifted off my spiritual eyes, and I could see the conditions of their hearts because they reflected the same need for repentance I had had.

I had begun to see my mom through adult (mature) eyes. I could see that her anger, bitterness, distance, and indifference really had nothing to do with me. It wasn't aimed at me, and it wasn't personal. I became full of compassion for her, and all my awkward and distant feelings toward her from my childhood fell off of me. I didn't need her to repent for my sake—she needed to repent for her own sake. As I brought her to more repentance, she was the one that benefitted the most as the oppression of guilt fell off of her.

I transferred my new mature thought processes about my mom over to my children and began to see them differently. I realized that I had been taking some of their resistance, distance, and disobedience personally. I had been responding to it like it was aimed at me so I became displeased and unhappy with my children. I showered them with disapproval and tried to shame them into behaving better, and I didn't feel like being affectionate when I was displeased with them.

Now I clearly saw that they were trapped in their sin, and God had a plan for them. It wasn't about me; it wasn't personal. My heart welled up with compassion for my children. I turned to the Lord and began to ask what He wanted to do in them, and I expected answers. I offered myself to the Lord fully to cooperate with His plan, confessing that I had not been paying attention in my self-centeredness. All thoughts of what my children were doing to me dropped out of my thinking in every way.

> *"I transferred my new mature thought processes about my mom over to my children and began to see them differently."*

I became free to pour love and affection on my children even when they were not doing as they ought because I knew it wasn't about me. My children's misbehavior became a topic of conversation between the Lord and me, and it had no effect on my love and affection toward them. They could no longer disappoint me, make me frustrated, make me feel disrespected, or panicked. I learned that they weren't producing those things inside me anyway. Those attitudes of my heart were coming from my own self-focused motivations.

My children's response to this new unconditional love coming from me was quick, and their hearts became melted into mine. The things the Lord led me to do with them made rapid, often instant, changes in their behavior.

Too many parents take up personal offense at their children's behavior. If we have to go and cool off before dealing with our children or we get frustrated and irritated, if we engage in conflict with them or are afraid of their responses, if we are complaining to our friends about our children's bad behavior and comfort each other that it's something normal we must all endure, then we are receiving our children's behavior as a personal offense. We are making their need for salvation and growth about ourselves, focusing on how their behavior affects us, robbing them of the ministry they need.

Some parents try to fool themselves into thinking that angry outbursts are for the benefit of their children so they can become better people, but it's just not true. Angry outbursts or frustrated lectures only prove that you still believe that life is all about you. We need to rise up and become mature. As Marilyn's *challenging idea #7* says, *"God wants to influence you toward heart-level change before you try to change your children—a top-down, inside-out approach provides understanding and wisdom for parenting...As God parents you, so parent your children."*

God has many miracles in mind for your family, and He's just waiting for you to repent, rise up in mature loving compassion for your children, offer yourself to Him, and follow His specific direction for winning their hearts and drawing them to Him.

Ministry to My Daughter, Rachel

My daughter, Rachel, who had just turned 14 years old at the time of Gramma's miraculous change, had developed a way of relating with her Gramma that was different from the rest of the kids.

Rachel's room was right next to Gramma's. This close proximity meant that Rachel was often the only responsible one around when Gramma was doing something potentially hazardous. If Gramma started wandering the house at night, it was Rachel who heard her. If she started rummaging through the bathroom cupboards it was Rachel who was usually closest by. If Gramma began to leave her room without enough clothes on Rachel was usually the first to spot it and try to stop her.

Since Gramma's general demeanor was so harsh and mean, Rachel had adopted a similar harsh and mean way of commanding her to do what she needed to do until I could come and take over. Rachel was met with all Gramma's spewing resentment, bared clenched teeth, shaking fists, and pounding on walls much more than the other kids, and she met it with a combination of strong fierceness and deep fear. Rachel remained stoic knowing that she was directing Gramma toward what was best for her, but she was frustrated knowing that Gramma would really only listen to me, even though Rachel was trying her best.

When Gramma was suddenly transformed into someone full of gratitude, smiles, and encouragement I could see that Rachel didn't know what to do with the big wall of self-protection that she had built up against

Gramma. I could see that she was bracing for all the meanness to come back. As we began to draw near to Gramma, spending time by her side, Rachel hung back. She was curious but confused. I knew I had to talk with her.

I don't remember what I said and what she said, but I remember that Rachel needed me to understand her and help her understand herself. I talked with her about how reasonable her feelings toward Gramma had been. It seems to me that we didn't talk much, but Rachel just crumbled into my arms crying as she released all the fear with long heaving sighs of relief. I talked with her about forgiving Gramma for the way she had treated her. I encouraged her to come a little closer when we talked with Gramma. I watched as Rachel made efforts to bring her walls down and accept the new Gramma.

> *"It was so shocking to us all and so graphic! We all had no doubt that the flesh was ugly, and the workings of God's Spirit were amazingly loving".*

We had many conversations about the difference between Gramma's flesh (her self-seeking nature) and her spirit, which was now free to love. It was so shocking to us all and so graphic! We all had no doubt that the flesh was ugly, and the workings of God's Spirit were amazingly loving. We couldn't help but search our own hearts, knowing that ugliness was hiding in there, and we all had a fervent desire to fling it far from us. Even the kids understood what the flesh was.

Being a very responsible firstborn, Rachel often found herself in a position of knowing what was best to be done and wanting to direct all the other kids toward that end. I had known for a long time that Rachel's way of ordering the other kids around had just too much of a harsh edge to it. I didn't like her tone of voice and the strength she put behind her commands to the other kids. I would sometimes try to direct her to speak more gently, but even when she spoke gently her commands carried the same bossy nature. I didn't know what to do, especially since Rachel was almost always right in what she was telling the younger kids to do.

> *"That harshness left Rachel that moment. She was changed from the inside out at the heart level."*

One sunny afternoon not long after Gramma's change, Rachel and I were down by the fire pit. Some of the other kids were there and Rachel commanded them to do something that was a good idea, and they went off in obedience. It suddenly dawned on me that Rachel's harshness was like Gramma's. I slowly explained to her that she sounded like the old Gramma when she talked like that to the kids. As I spoke I saw realization and conviction cross her face (a sight I've become very familiar with) and then just as quickly godly sorrow washed over her for the way she'd been treating her siblings. Brokenness wrinkled her face up into tears of repentance. She heaved out, "I never want to be like Gramma was to the kids! She scared me so much and I never want to do that to them again!"

That harshness left Rachel that moment. She was changed from the inside out at the heart level. Rachel quickly adopted my new unconditional love for the kids, and they responded to her as well by melting their hearts into hers.

My Daughter, Annie, Is Reconciled

As we got used to Gramma being changed from being completely self-absorbed, grouchy, and ignoring everyone to being completely aware, encouraging, and connected to everyone around her, I began to spend time every now and then throughout our days sitting beside her to engage in conversation. I would pull the younger kids up into my lap so they could get used to being close to Gramma.

Our conversations went something like this. She would say, "I wear glasses....This boy wears glasses," as she pointed to Josiah. I would say, "That's Josiah." She would repeat his name several times, smile at him, and then wave to him. Then she would say, "I wear glasses... He wears glasses too." I would tell her his name again, and she'd repeat it over and over. We'd go 'round and 'round like this for a while.

Sometimes we would give her a picture of herself when she was about 20 years old. She would carefully explain to us who was in the picture. Sometimes she said it was her mother, sometimes she said it was herself. We would often ask how old she was in the picture, and how old she was now. She would say, "Oh, that was about 10 years ago....I think I'm about 35 now." It was always a different answer which would make us all laugh, which would make her laugh and laugh. She would begin to get goofy and wink at the kids, pointing to them with nothing particular to say but to giggle and wave. Occasionally asking their names. She'd end up saying, "I wear glasses...so does he."

As we had funny conversations with Gramma, I began to notice that any time Gramma looked in Annie's direction, Annie would look away. She remained close to the visiting, but would not meet Gramma's eyes. I began to pray about Annie's response to Gramma. I felt like Annie needed to forgive Gramma for the way she had been—harsh, mean, and scary.

> *"Tears started rolling down Annie's cheeks. I hugged her and asked her if she could forgive Gramma. She nodded and cried."*

One sunny day I invited Annie to take a walk with me. We walked up and down the road above our house arm in arm. I explained to her that she probably had some resistance against Gramma because Gramma had been treating her badly. I told her that I saw that she didn't want to look into Gramma's eyes. Annie was very quiet. I told her that she could let Gramma be a new person. She could forgive Gramma and let her start over with a new way of relating.

Tears started rolling down Annie's cheeks. I hugged her and asked her if she could forgive Gramma. She nodded and cried.

The next time we were all gathered around Gramma, I watched as Annie disciplined herself to meet Gramma's eyes, and then she disciplined herself to return Gramma's smile. Once she saw that she could let go of the resistance against her, she quickly melted into enjoying the new Gramma with the rest of us.

Marilyn's *challenging idea #3* says, *"It's impossible to transfer moral values in broad generalities that are unrelational. They are successfully instilled only by addressing the particulars of your family's relating habits and patterns."* In the past, in my flesh, I couldn't even see Rachel's harsh behavior toward Gramma, and Annie's resistance because their particular morality (relational habits) matched my own. Once I changed, I could see how my kids needed the same change, and the Holy Spirit gave me the wisdom to show them how by addressing their particular relating habits and patterns.

More Reconciliation

Soon I was able to talk and pray with my mom about her relationship with her father who had died many years before. As I prayed about her lack of affection, I received direction from the Holy Spirit to talk with her about her relationship with him. During our conversation, she suddenly and forcefully declared that she hated her father, which I had not known before. She spoke many things with intense bitterness and resentment and she slammed her fists on the arms of her chair and gnashed her teeth. I was encouraging her to forgive him, but she stubbornly struggled with that idea saying that she didn't think she could, and she didn't want to. She continued rehearsing her bitter memories and her hate, but finally, she took a deep breath and slumped down letting go of her defiant posture, "OK," she said, "I'll forgive him." I helped her to pray and she began to weep. She repented of holding on to all that bitterness, hatred, and anger.

Just moments later she told me that if she had grandchildren, she would hug them and love them and hold them close. I told her she did have grandchildren, and then I told her the truth about how she used to treat them and she began weeping again desperately wanting to know if she could ask their forgiveness. I called the kids into her room and as they filed in, she stood and reached out to them. She took each of their faces in her hands one at a time and looked into their eyes, weeping and asking their forgiveness, which they freely gave. She pulled them all into a big group hug.

I could easily fill a book with the changes that took place after this. As the kids and I sat and laughed with her, she would take the hand of whoever was sitting next to her and affectionately rub it as long as they stayed. She began coming close to us whenever we were gathered talking, especially around our bar as I cooked meals. She didn't want to be left out of conversation, and she would sometimes wander into the kitchen asking for hugs from everyone. She watched our activities with great concentration, speaking out encouragement to everyone in their efforts, and rehearsing the kids' names.

> *"She began coming close to us whenever we were gathered talking, especially around our bar as I cooked meals."*

The younger kids found out that Gramma loved playing "peek-a-boo." They would pop out from behind things and say, "Gramma!", and duck back again. She just laughed and laughed. The older kids discovered that they could tell her the same joke over and over and each time she cracked up hysterically, not remembering that she just heard the same joke only moments ago. The all-time favorite though was when the kids gave Gramma a toy rifle. She really got into character and shot at the kids as they shot back, ducking and hiding. When they would pretend to die with great drama because of her superior shooting, she would laugh herself into tears and breathlessness. Because of her total lack of short-term memory, she never got tired of the fun. She never knew how long she'd been playing and laughing, and each moment was new.

Another Journal Entry

This morning while we were talking about heaven, Gramma declared that she wasn't ready to go there yet. When asked what she wanted to do first she said, "I want to enjoy my grandchildren!"

Below is what Rachel and Annie dictated about Gramma to be read at her memorial service. It took Annie a long time to dictate hers because she was weeping so much as she spoke of her fondness for Gramma.

Rachel, September 2009—"I liked how Grandma always had a smile, a wave, or applause for all the musical things I did in her presence. I was so blessed by her love of the music I made. As her condition worsened, I needed to help my mom with Gramma more and more. I'm thankful that I had the opportunity to learn how to love her, without expecting anything in return. I learned how to be patient, kind, and loving, even though sometimes I had already told her the same thing ten times. I always felt blessed when she smiled at me, patted my hand, or acknowledged that I was her helper."

Annie, September 2009—"Gramma was always ready to give everybody a smile. Whenever we were doing something she wanted to get involved too. She wanted to be with us. Whenever we were laughing, she would laugh even if she didn't know why we were laughing. Whenever we told a funny joke, Gramma would laugh really hard and say, "You're a nut!" even if she heard the joke over and over again. Sometimes she would forget what she was going to say, and so she would end by saying something that was really funny, and when we laughed, she would laugh. Gramma taught us to be unselfish because we had to give up a lot to take care of her. We couldn't go to a lot of places, and sometimes we couldn't stay very long because we had to get her home. That has made it easier for me to give up other things. Gramma liked to hear me sing, and she would smile at me, or even sing along. When Gramma couldn't talk much anymore she would "purr" at me."

My Relationship with Marilyn and More Understanding of Repentance

Over the weeks of this miraculous process, Marilyn continued to talk with me about more of my wrong ways of thinking and relating. For example, I had experienced deep rejection from several mom-type people in my life starting with my own mom. Marilyn seemed to me to be a mom-type person and so I was automatically afraid that she would reject me too. I treated her like I was afraid of her, and I believed she was rejecting me in some of the things she had done and said. In truth-telling, she pointed out to me how I was doing this, and then she let me know that it was very unloving. It was hurtful to put my past experiences on her and relate to her as though she was just the same as the others. I was not allowing her to be who she is but assuming she was and would continue to be something else. I was protecting myself against my imagination of her, and it was unloving.

> *"It was hurtful to put my past experiences on her and relate to her as though she was just the same as the others. I was protecting myself against my imagination of her, and it was unloving."*

This made sense to me, and I was very sorry for treating her that way. I wasn't just sorry, I was filled with sorrow. It was obvious to me that she was sacrificially pouring out her life for me and my mom, and the last thing I wanted to do was be hurtful to her. My sorrow was over the way I was hurting her with my behavior while she was loving me so. I actually saw that the reasons I thought she was rejecting me were only coming from inside of me. I had imagined them, and that made me even more sorrowful because she was blameless, while I had mistreated her. I became truly repentant, and it was accompanied by a *complete* lack of desire to ever do that to her again.

So many believers don't actually know what true repentance is. True repentance must be focused on the hurt caused to another and their well-being. In my sorrow, I wasn't sorry that I'd messed up, and I wasn't embarrassed for being exposed in it. Those thoughts would be about me. I did not try to figure out how to hide my fear of her better. I did not try to stop the behaviors that accompanied my fear so that she would think I got rid of it. That would be about me. I didn't try to be a better friend so that she wouldn't have to think those things about me. That would be about me. I did not try to push away my fearful thoughts or ignore them, because they simply did not exist anymore.

I was being truthful in recognizing my sin for what it was. I switched from protection for myself to concern for her. I was concerned about the way she felt at my treatment, and so I connected with the real her in my repentance. My concern for the *real* her (the one that was not rejecting me) transformed me. This experience in connecting with Marilyn on a *real* level prepared me for another real connection—with God.

My Understanding of the Ministry of Reconciliation

As it became more and more obvious that the miraculous changes in my mom, in me, and in my children were not going to "wear off", and the changes only became deeper as I learned to meet their soul and spirit needs, I began to invite other people to come and see. I wanted to tell people about it. I struggled with expressing what was actually happening. I felt like words that I'd heard my whole life in church settings and in the Bible suddenly meant something different than what I'd always thought.

I don't remember the circumstances, but one day early on, my eyes fell on a verse in 2 Corinthians:

> "...*God, Who through Jesus Christ reconciled us to Himself....*
> *and gave to us the ministry of reconciliation.*"
> 2 Corinthians 5:18-19

The Message Bible says it like this:

"We're Christ's representatives. God uses us to persuade men and women to drop their differences and enter into God's work of making things right between them."

It was then that I saw so clearly in this verse what was happening all around my life. It was reconciliation. My mom was being reconciled to me, to God, and toward her long-deceased father. I was leading my children to be reconciled with Gramma, and with each other. Marilyn was leading me to be reconciled with my mom, and with herself. I was being led by the Holy Spirit through my conscience to be reconciled with my children. All around me, all these awesome changes were coming because people were being reconciled to people.

At the same time, I was dwelling upon a principle of relationship that Marilyn had taught during the meetings at her house the fall before, in 2005. She had said that the beginning of any relationship is an investment of interest in the other. In order to begin or build *any* relationship we must become interested in what the other is interested in, and make those interests our own—this is the *beginning* of building or fixing relationship. The Lord brought these two thoughts together for me in a way that suddenly and radically changed my life from the inside out.

Connecting with the REAL Him

I was walking on the road above our house listening to worship music, and overflowing with thanks toward the Lord for all He was doing, when it suddenly occurred to me that I, as a believer, was supposed to have a *ministry of reconciliation,* which meant that all my effort and activity in life needed to point toward seeing people be reconciled with each other. Then I realized that this is what interested God—reconciliation. I saw that the beginning of my relationship with Him would be to take on this interest of His as my own and make it my interest, my concern, my focus. He had already given His Son Jesus to die for me. Now it was my turn to become interested in what interested Him to make our relationship two-sided and bring it to maturity.

Suddenly I had a revelation of what I had been spending the effort and activity of my life on. It wasn't reconciliation. I *thought* I had been living my life for Him. I believed I was. I intended to be. But I suddenly saw I had been thinking that His plan was to get people to come to church and to like being there so they could become church people and adopt spiritual disciplines like daily personal devotions, Bible study, and commitment to church activity. This had been my understanding of what it meant to serve God.

> *"I was overcome with sorrow at how I'd served this false image of God. I had assumed things about Him and what He values that were not true of Him at all. I began heaving with tears, sobs, and unintelligible cries of repentance."*

It takes a lot longer to write this out, but I saw it all suddenly in my heart and mind. It was an unveiling. I realized that in all my years of "serving God" I had not even begun to build my relationship with the *real* Him, because I was mistaken about what He was actually interested in and concerned about. I realized that I hadn't even *known* Him, and I was spending my life effort and activity in service to my *idea* of Him, instead of the *real* Him.

I was overcome with sorrow at how I'd served this false image of God. I had assumed things about Him and what He values that were not true of Him at all, while He had sacrificed so much for me. I began heaving with tears, sobs, and unintelligible cries of repentance. I was just as thoroughly overcome with waves of forgiveness and acceptance, totally experiencing His LOVE. I don't know how long I just stood there on the road under my neighbor's cedar tree. It felt like a long time where the Lord and I were speaking to each other at the same time. I was surrendering my whole life to serving the real Him, and taking on His true interests and concerns as my own. He was showering me with acceptance, love, approval, and assurance as well as a deeper understanding of what was happening. I can't speak of this meeting with the Lord without falling apart in tears of gratitude that come from so deep I have to resist the pressure of convulsing with emotion.

My sorrow was about how hurtful I had been to the Lord. I was repenting and *connecting* with the *real* Him, and my desire for my fleshly ways was gone from me. He transformed me and filled me full of His love as I was connecting and relating with the real Him. As Marilyn's *challenging idea #6* says, *"God gives us the Law of Love, a powerful tool to accomplish two practical purposes—to know ourselves and to know Him."* As I learned to love the people in my life, I was drawn toward loving Him. I became aware of my true condition and abandoned my wrong ideas of Him as I came to know the REAL Him.

Freedom from the Grip of the Flesh

When others hear my testimony of reconciliation in my family, I've known some to say to me,

"Barbie, it doesn't sound like you were really struggling. I've been trying to be loving to my family, but it's so hard! I have to fight against my fleshly self-centered ways day in and day out. I'm so tired, and some days I just fall back into all the ugliness I have inside toward my children, and then I become afraid that I haven't even changed at all."

It's true. I struggled against my self-centered ways only for about two to three weeks. My struggle was not against ugly behaviors toward my children but against resistance toward my mom. I willingly chose to do loving things for my mom while inside I did not feel like doing them. I did not have loving feelings or desires. I swallowed hard and felt sick in my stomach as I smiled into my mom's eyes, and held her hands, inviting her to pray with me. I knew my feelings were wrong, and I knew they were based on a lifetime of my wrong responses to her. I was choosing to do the right thing on the outside but I did not have the feelings to match it on the inside. After my experience with the Lord that day under the cedar tree, I came away totally changed at my core. All the fleshly self-centered ways of thinking and feeling that I was aware of were gone from me, and I *never* struggled against them again.

My struggle ceased because my repentance was true. It was about how I had wrongly been treating God. I was not sorry and disappointed that I'd been missing it. I was not planning how I would be a better Christian. I was not kicking myself and wishing I hadn't been spending my life on the wrong things. I was not thinking that He must think I was really dumb. That would be all about me. I was not planning how to get busy with the activities of reconciliation so that I wouldn't be missing it anymore. These takes on the situation would have been about me.

If you're constantly being tempted to obey your self-centered ways even though you see them fully, then perhaps you haven't actually repented. You haven't actually become sorrowful over how you're treating your family and God Himself, and your efforts toward right behavior, even your attempts to say you're sorry are actually, in the deepest part of you, all about you. If you haven't entered into the pain you've caused another; if your idea of repentance is all about you, then you aren't actually relating and connecting with the real person you've wronged or the *real Him*, and I suggest your repentance may not be true. It's your *real* relationship with others and with Him that He's after. Merely being a good parent and a nice, sincere person falls far short of true repentance and it falls short of His desire for relationship with the *real you*.

> "The reason the struggle ceased is because my repentance was true. It was about how I had wrongly been treating God."

What is your motivation for being a loving parent? Is it so you can have a successful family? Is it so you can prove that you are good? Are you trying to prove it to yourself or to God or to your own parent? Are you trying to save yourself from the embarrassment of having rebellious teens? Are you trying to do what God seems to want, so He will accept you? All these are self-serving motivations and there are millions more. They all lead to self-service even though the outward actions appear to be good and loving. Why are you trying to be loving? Is it because you want to be holy as He is holy? Do you want to identify with Christ more than anything or anyone else, including your own false personality?

Are you taking on God's interests as your own? Are you fully surrendered to His work of reconciliation in your family? Are you cooperating with His leadings through your conscience to relate rightly with your family, and lead them to follow your example, entering into His plan for reconciliation with Him, and receiving His call on your life to minister reconciliation to your family? Or do you have another idea of what serving God looks like?

Gramma Is Reconciled to the Rest of Her Family

I wrote of the changes in my mom to my sisters and invited them to come and see for themselves. Before they came, I sat and prayed and talked with her about some of the circumstances of our childhood. Again she became very lucid and talked with me for an hour and a half! She recounted how her bitterness toward her father caused her to treat her daughters with indifference and neglect. She talked about how she let other people hurt us and how she let others control her. After we prayed and cried and she repented, she turned to me and said, "I was a *real mess*!!" She asked if there was any way she could apologize to her other daughters. When I told her they were coming soon, she asked me repeatedly to help her remember that she wanted to ask for their forgiveness. When my sisters came, they were shocked and amazed just as my family and I had been. Her whole being was radically changed. She asked for their forgiveness as she confessed to all of us her bitterness, distance, and neglect, and she showered us with hugs.

Gramma's flesh wasn't any uglier than all of ours. The disease left her without the ability to cover it up with a socially acceptable veneer. Your family has seen your flesh though, and they've felt it too. Won't you fling it far from you and come to repentance? Won't you let down your walls of self-protection and pride and begin to delight in others, giving and receiving love? Won't you allow the Lord to convict you so you can be changed from the inside out?

Gramma Is Reconciled to Jesus

A few weeks later, I sat and talked with my mom about Jesus. I asked her to tell me about her relationship with Him. She took a deep breath and looked right in my eyes and said, "I have been running from Jesus my whole life." I helped her to pray and ask Jesus to forgive her for running, and she told Him she didn't want to run anymore. She told Jesus that she wanted to run toward Him, which is where she is now. She finished the race.

Some of you may be asking, "How can someone so involved in church service and ministry have been running from Jesus?" In every outward appearance, my mom was pursuing Jesus, not running from Him. She truly did have a desire for the things of the Lord and she truly had the desire to help people with the help of the Lord. She believed that He had the answers to life's difficulties. She prayed and studied the things of God, trying to understand His ways, and passing on what she'd read to others.

> *"You see, the evidence of our need for reconciliation with God is revealed in our human relationships..."*

The part of her life where she was running from God was in her habits of relating. You see, *the evidence of our need for reconciliation with God is revealed in our human relationships,* but she did not allow God's transforming power to touch her there. When we hold the faults that we believe others have in a package of criticism, judgment, bitterness, and resentment, we are running from Jesus. When we hold our family members at an emotional distance, withholding affection and friendly concern, we are running from Jesus. Irritation, outbursts of anger, and taking up offense at people, especially our family members, are all symptoms of a need for reconciliation with God. My mom did not understand what God wanted to accomplish in her. She was not actually experiencing the Love of Jesus, and so she did not have Jesus' kind of love to pour on her family, which resulted in the alienation and distance that I've written about.

The Apostle Paul says,

> *"The object and purpose of our instruction and charge is love, which springs from a pure heart and a good (clear) conscience and sincere (unfeigned) faith."*
> 1 Timothy 1:5

We actually experience the Love of Jesus when we run toward having a pure heart and a clear conscience in our relationships. Are thoughts of the state of your relationships coming to your mind? Are you seeing in your relationships the symptoms of a need for reconciliation? Conviction of conscience is often uncomfortable, sometimes even distressing. It can make us feel like pushing these thoughts away and burying them back where they were before. But don't. I hope and pray that you don't run from Jesus and the work of reconciliation that He wants to accomplish in all of our lives.

Scripture tells us to,

> *"Search for peace (harmony; undisturbedness from moral (which is relational) conflicts) and seek it eagerly. [Do not merely desire peaceful relations with God, with your fellowmen, and with yourself, but pursue, go after them!]."*
> 1 Peter 3:11

It means we need to do more than wish we had peaceful and loving relationships. We need to search, seek eagerly, pursue, and go after reconciliation with the people in our life.

Running to Jesus

God can see the attitudes and motivations of your heart that you direct toward others and His desire is to shower you with forgiveness and His love. This is what happened to my mom; this is her testimony. This is the message of reconciliation that 2 Corinthians 5 is talking about. As she repented to me, to her grandchildren, to my sisters, to God, she became full of the Love of Jesus, and it overflowed onto us every day. It overflowed onto everyone who came around her in these last few years. The alienation, distance, and estrangement were completely gone, and replaced with affection, favor, and goodwill.

Because of my mom's reconciliation, we began to understand what God actually wanted to accomplish in us. We began to search our relationships for alienation, loss of affection, being controlled by others, and wrong attitudes and motivations, and we ran toward reconciliation. We ran toward Jesus as we had never known before. I could go on and on about what the love and forgiveness of Jesus have accomplished in my family and in my husband too.

God is interested in your reconciliation with the people in your life, starting with your family. Will you take up His interests as your own, run to Jesus, meet the real Him, and repent? Will you receive His generous grace and forgiveness? Will you become a parent who is full of the love of Jesus and regularly showers it on your children, meeting their soul and spirit needs and blessing them?

In Memory of Ellen Spencer Connett

May 14, 1927 - September 10, 2009
And in Praise and Glory to Jesus Christ!
~ the mediator of reconciliation and the giver of life ~

The Overcoming Life

People learn from a young age to put up a false image for others so they don't have to be known as their real selves. This "false personality" is just their flesh baggage that was never dealt with. However, these long-term fleshly habits of relating are strongholds that people themselves rarely are able to see without help from a loving person who is interested in their freedom. A stronghold is simply a controlling or dominant behavior trait that comes to affect all areas of the person's life and all close relationships with a spouse and children, preventing the person's true spiritual growth. Controlling traits are like the tentacles of an octopus that reach into all relational situations and suck the life out of them. When exposed and dealt with, the person is able to effectively "crush the head" of the octopus and the tentacles simply let go, shrivel up and die, leaving the relationship clear for the fruit of the Spirit to grow in all the areas that previously had been strangled and closed off.

> *"And he who overcomes*
> *(is victorious) and who obeys*
> *My commands to the [very] end*
> *[doing the works that please Me],*
> *I will give him authority and*
> *power over the nations."*
> *~ Revelation 2:26*

When friendships don't provide an opportunity for real relationships to develop, a person's fleshly relational habits and patterns can seem barely noticeable to the casual observer, but close family members are acutely aware of the problems. And so, when a spouse becomes free of controlling behaviors that prevent intimacy in a marriage or prevent the family from the happiness and joy in the Lord He promises to believers, it is nothing less than a miracle. The entire dynamic of the family home atmosphere and relational environment changes toward Christlike love. This is what happened in the Poling family. *God wants you to be free to LOVE!*

Here is a list of the strongholds from which Jesus set Tim and Barbie Poling free. We give glory to God for the powerful works of reconciliation He accomplished in their family and the growing Christlike character and love that comes from Him alone.

> ***Tim*** ~ anger, blameshifting, criticalness, judgmentalism, pride, supreme arrogance, compulsive behavior, religious duty, controlling others, deceit, insecurity, and intentional withholding of love.
>
> ***Barbie*** ~ rejection, misplaced concern, self-judgmentalism, desire to be controlled, religious duty, messiness, using people, fear of confrontation, twisted thinking, love of knowledge.

It was my joy to witness both Tim and Barbie confess in tears and remorse on many occasions over the hurts they caused their family and each other and even me. They both became authentic Christians who know how to love God and others. Tim and Barbie have a close loving relationship today, and as a father, Tim worked soberly to win back the hearts of his two oldest children and continues to strengthen the heart bonds with all of his children. While Barbie helps me personally with a multitude of inglorious tasks related to ministry and business, Tim works right alongside her quick to give and serve generously from the heart to meet many real needs in our faith community. Their children are also completely involved in the work of the ministry with them. Tim and Barbie are true friends to the whole Howshall family and co-laborers in Christ to our ever-growing faith community. We are so grateful the Lord is sharing them with us.

Let The Bells Ring! ~ A Call to Assembly

Bells have always signified a call to assembly—to warn and inform. This message is like the sounding of a bell, lovingly warning you about the potential loss of spiritual and relational fruit, and informing you of actions to take now to become better parents who successfully transfer God's moral values and faith to their children. We can learn how to parent as God parents us. God is calling us to action! Let the bells ring for assembly, in every home, in every church, in every Christian school, and in every community across this land. Let the call go forth again and again and yet again. Let it be repeated in every church bulletin, every Sunday, in every adult Sunday School class, in every fellowship hall, and in every Pastor's sermon. Let the bells sound for your children need you, and time doesn't stand still. God is calling you, and He is longing to help you. Let every caring Christian parent arise and assume your proper position. Rise to the challenge of allowing God to parent you so you can disciple your children for Him, and reverse the trend of apostasy sweeping this land. You can answer this call; you must answer this call; your children's future depends upon it! Your children need you! God will enable you with His own plan. You can do this. You must do this! Let it be, Lord! Let the bells ring!

Information

Sign the Declaration—It Starts With Me

We believe you've experienced an awakening as you've read this book. It's an awakening about "We The Parents..." addressing family governance and how the family is educated and discipled. It's all about the children. We can no longer let our children's character training be left to chance.

We invite you to ItStartsWithMeMovement.com to sign the following declaration along with many other parents who have realized changes are needed.

Declaration

We The Parents, in order to form a more spiritually unified FAMILY and CHURCH, establish righteousness, and relationally disciple and educate our children in God's ways, do hereby covenant with our Heavenly Father to be parented by Him, to learn how to parent as He parents us, to learn how to meet our children's soul-felt needs, and love them as God loves us, to raise them up for the glory of Jesus Christ.

As a parent, I declare that it starts with me. I will endeavor, by the grace of God, to receive God's correction and instruction to my heart in His ways so that as God parents me, I will be empowered to parent my children for Him.

It Starts with Me

We invite you to join us on Facebook at https://www.facebook.com/MarilynHowshall.FHM

'Empowered Hearts Ministry' app is free and available on Google Play and the Apple app store.

If this message has ministered to your heart and need, we pray it is only the beginning of many answered prayers for you and your family.

— Please consider sharing this message with others by passing on our website information.

— Please leave a review on Amazon.

We thank you and bless you with God's richest spiritual blessings in Jesus Christ.

Empowering the Heartbeat of Your Life
www.marilynhowshall.com

Glossary Appendix

"...I will put My law within them, and on their HEARTS will I write it; and I will be their God, and they will be My people."

Jeremiah 31:33

"HEART" The place of God's work in our lives; where the quality of our relational habits are formed, which forms our character; the stage on which intimate relationship with God and with people is acted out; the seat of conscience; our attitudes, intentions, and motivations.

"DISCIPLESHIP" The process of reconciling our lives and relationships to Christ at the heart-level, becoming a true follower of Him and His ways.

"GOD'S PLACE OF INFLUENCE IN OUR LIVES" Our morality—human relational patterns of behavior.

"CHARACTER" The sum of our relational habits.

"MORALITY" The quality of how we relate with each other.

"PARTICULAR MORALITY" How we treat another in the particulars of our habits; how we communicate and solve conflicts and misunderstandings.

"MORAL CHOICES" How we choose to relate with others.

"MORAL BEHAVIOR" The quality of our habitual patterns of relating.

"MORAL DECISIONS" The conscious or subconscious relational decisions for how we will relate with another.

"QUALITY OF OUR MORALITY" The love or unlove in which we relate with each other.

"SANCTIFYING PROCESS" The ongoing work of the Holy Spirit in our hearts to bring us into Christlikeness.

"ACQUAINTANCE" Familiar and intimate knowledge (more than slight or superficial).

"INTIMATE RELATIONSHIPS" Where particular correction and instruction are lovingly given and gladly received so that our hearts and lives may embody Christ's Law of Love. Where anything can be talked through to mutual understanding and satisfaction in knowing and being known; depth of knowledge and understanding of each other.

"ACQUAINTED WITH CHRIST'S LAW OF LOVE" Familiar and intimate knowledge of His standards for our relationships and our relational interchanges.

"ACQUAINTANCE WITH SIN" Familiarity and intimate knowledge of our own particular, self-seeking relational patterns so we can work toward repentance, and build our faith (working through love) toward the developing of holy character [the sum of our relational habits].

"TEACHING" Usually the transfer of knowledge through the communication of words; mostly general theory.

"INSTRUCTION" The transfer of personalized knowledge by one to another through the communication of words, but carried through a spirit of love that provides specific insights to aid in the transfer of principles into real-life situations and relationships.

"THE RELATIONAL ACTIVITY OF THE HOLY SPIRIT" He convicts and judges of sin and He convicts of righteousness; He corrects, instructs and comforts us in the Lord's ways of Love. He judges and convicts us of our fruit.

"RIGHTEOUSNESS" Moral and spiritual rectitude; right living in loving relationship with God and with others.

"MORAL AND SPIRITUAL RECTITUDE" The quality of our love in our relations with God and with others that puts us in right standing with them, and makes us righteous.

"WANT OF RECTITUDE" Sinful and debasing; lack of love and right relating.

"LIVING IN SELF-WILL" Cut off from experiencing God's love and acceptance; living a life of using and taking, self-centeredness, stinginess of relationship.

"LIVING IN GOD'S WILL" Experiencing His love and acceptance; living a life of serving, sharing and giving; generosity of heart.

"SIN" A self-centered failure to love.

"WHERE SIN BEGINS" In the attitudes, intentions, and motivations of the heart.

"ATTITUDE" The thought processes or emotional posture that expresses the sentiments and actions of the person in response to life's situations and challenges.

"INTENTION" The earnest bending of the mind that determines action and manner; having designs, purposes or desired outcomes for a behavior toward ourselves and others.

"MOTIVATION" The driving force or reasons for a particular behavior toward a desired outcome. The reason or "why we do and say what we do and say."

"HOLY" Purely loving.

"THE MORAL LAW OF LOVE" Christ's two new commandments of love—the quality of our attitudes, intentions, and motivations with God and with others.

"LOVE" Self-sacrificial qualities in the attitudes, intentions, and motivations of the heart that translate into actions toward God and others.

"WALKING IN LOVE" Intentionally taking specific love actions as explicitly commanded in the Scriptures, and by the Holy Spirit's instruction to the conscience.

"RELATING IN LOVE" Developing sacrificial moral qualities in attitudes, intentions, and motivations toward others.

"The Law of Love" The New Commandment that Jesus gave; the command that sums up all the Law and the Prophets; a powerful tool to accomplish two practical purposes—to know ourselves and to know Him.

"adherence to The Law" A matter of the selfless, sacrificial quality of our heart as it's outworked in our relationships.

"The Law of Liberty" A term comprehensive of all Scripture (James 1:25). It is not a law of compulsion enforced from without, but it is a law out of desire and delight of the renewed heart that has truly experienced the living Christ through the inner workings of the Holy Spirit. The believer is ready to obey, and willingly and eagerly puts himself under Christ's Law of Love. It's aptly named because the believer who has responded to the workings of the Holy Spirit—as the disciples did—is now free from self-centeredness, and at Liberty to simply love (2 Corinthians 3:17).

"fleshly behavior" A carnal response or reaction of self-will that's perhaps caused by a legitimate condition of our life, but where we have a choice in how to respond. In every case, we are breaking God's Moral Law of Love.

"flesh" Self-centered ways and behavior practices that oppose God (that prevent us from knowing Him and produce bad spiritual fruit).

"False personality" Our habitual, unloving relational habits.

"DEAD WORKS" False religious standards of righteousness or self-generated relational habits (substitute actions, behaviors, and activities) that take the place of living God's love through us, according to His standards of righteousness.

"WICKED" To wind, turn, depart, or fall away. Any practice deviating from the Divine Law of Love, and extending to everything that is contrary to right relating, and leads to corruption and perversion of heart and mind.

"EVIL" Bad qualities of a moral kind that tend to corrupt and pervert.

"WHERE PERVERSION BEGINS" Perversion does not begin in the mind, but it begins in the heart with the quality of our morality [heart-level relating practices]. Our relating practices will either align us correctly with the Father or turn us away from Him to devise error that supports fleshly habits and patterns of relating so we don't have to repent (Matthew 15:18).

"BORN AGAIN" Trusting Christ's salvation from your sin, and cooperating with the work of His influence in your heart.

"If you confess with your mouth the Lord Jesus, and believe in your heart that God has raised Him from the dead, you will be saved."

Romans 10:9

Scripture Appendix

Deuteronomy 6:3—Chapter 7
Deuteronomy 6:6-7—Chapter 7
2 Chronicles 7:14—Chapter 5
Daniel 4:27—Chapter 2
Isaiah 5:18; 20-21—Chapter 5
Isaiah 26:7—Chapter 2
Isaiah 55:8—Chapter 3
Psalms 106:20—Chapter 5
Proverbs 22:6—Chapter 8
Matthew 5:8—Chapter 6
Matthew 5:28—Chapter 2
Matthew 6:33—Chapter 2
Matthew 7:13-14—Chapter 8
Matthew 11:28—Chapter 7
Matthew 15:18—Chapter 5
Matthew 22:37-40—Chapters 2, 6
Mark 10:42-43—Chapter 5
John 5:39—Chapter 5
John 5:39-40—Chapter 5
Romans 2:29—Chapter 7
Romans 3:20—Chapter 6
Romans 7:18—Chapter 6
Romans 10:9-10—Chapter 7
2 Corinthians 1:24—Chapter 5

2 Corinthians 3:16—Chapter 5
2 Corinthians 3:17—Chapter 5
2 Corinthians 5:18-19—Chapters 6, 9
2 Corinthians 13:5—Chapter 6
Galatians 3:28—Chapter 5
Galatians 5:6—Chapters 6, 7
Galatians 6:7—Chapter 1
Ephesians 6:14—Chapter 2
Philippians 1:9—Chapter 4
Philippians 1:9-11—Chapters 4, 8
Philippians 2:12-13—Chapter 6
Colossians 3:12-17—Chapter 8
1 Timothy 1:5—Chapter 9
1 Timothy 1:5-6—Chapter 4
2 Timothy 3:5—Chapter 2
Hebrews 8:6—Chapters 2, 5
Hebrews 8:10-12—Chapter 7
Hebrews 9:14—Chapter 6
Hebrews 10:14-18—Chapter 7
James 1:25—Chapter 5
1 Peter 3:11—Chapters 5, 9
2 Peter 1:5—Chapter 5
1 John 3:6—Chapter 6

Author's Biography

Marilyn and Jim Howshall, co-founded Lifestyle of Learning™ Ministries in 1990, and they have served the homeschool community full-time since then. Marilyn wrote a number of books, beginning with *Wisdom's Way of Learning* in 1994. This opened up speaking opportunities as an invited featured speaker at several state conventions, but she did most of her speaking at 2-day conferences with her husband and women's retreats she held throughout the country for fifteen years.

Since 2012 she has ministered primarily out of the message of her most recent work, *Empowered—Healing the Heartbeat of Your Family*. Her life is devoted to helping parents write (or rewrite) their best possible family story—to learn how to love and build whole family relationships through the Lord's ministry of reconciliation. Her passion is helping parents become emotionally and relationally fit so they will succeed in Biblical parenting. She also likes to mobilize wives to become true helpers to their husbands, so dads can heal their influence with their children. She dispenses practical wisdom that transforms lives and the relational culture of the home.

The Lord sent other families to surround her ministry and a church community was born by the Spirit. As an ordained minister, she now prayerfully oversees two dozen families as part of her ongoing local ministry.

The Howshalls have four children and three in-loves, and a growing group of precious grandchildren they eagerly help out with whenever they can. Living in the great Northwest surrounded by family and dear friends, they look forward to any opportunity to enjoy God's amazing creation with their favorite people.

Made in United States
Troutdale, OR
12/06/2023